LAWRENCE ZARIAN'S

10

COMMANDMENTS

FOR A **PERFECT**
WARDROBE

Note to Readers

"Lawrence is the go-to style guru every woman wishes she had on her speed dial. Luckily for me, I have him on mine! This book will give everyone the best shortcuts to finding their inner fashion star, as only Lawrence can tell it."
—LISA GREGORISCH - DEMPSEY, SENIOR EXECUTIVE PRODUCER, "EXTRA"

"No one's better at showing women how to 'take a hard left to sexy town' than Lawrence Zarian. He's a fashion superstar and his book, *10 Commandments for a Perfect Wardrobe,* is a MUST for every woman!"
—ALEX DUDA, EXECUTIVE PRODUCER, "THE STEVE HARVEY SHOW"

"Lawrence Zarian delivers *10 Commandments for a Perfect Wardrobe* without breaking his golden rule—kindness. Why I love Lawrence (and why audiences of millions do too) is that he shares his pearls of style wisdom without talking down to people. He pours himself into these pages and in doing so, he entertains, educates, enlightens, and most importantly, empowers."
—BRAD BESSEY, EXECUTIVE PRODUCER, "THE INSIDER"

"A delightful, informative read! It shows what I have known for over 10 years of having witnessed Lawrence's work in our Macy's By Appointment offices as he created his magical makeovers for women of all description. His talent, wit, and grace make the process a completely joyful experience for all involved."
—LINDA LEE, GROUP VICE PRESIDENT,
MACY'S PERSONAL SHOPPING & CORPORATE SALES

"I will always treasure the time in NYC when Lawrence made me over. The instantaneous bond of friendship coupled with his anointed gift of 'putting it all together' gave me the confidence to embrace life with style. Thank you for showing us all how it's done and doing it with love."
—LUCY LONG, WIFE & MOTHER, MEMPHIS, TN
(MARRIED 33 YEARS WITH ONE SON)

"I have worked with Lawrence since he first got his start on camera and have watched him successfully continue to entertain and inform legions of women in a language that's both accessible and aspirational. This, along with his passion for fashion and compassion for his clients, is why he resonates with audiences everywhere. *10 Commandments for a Perfect Wardrobe* is a natural extension of Lawrence's impressive body of work and an absolute 'must-have' for every woman who wants to look and feel great—inside and out."

—LAUREN BLINCOE, VICE PRESIDENT, CURRENT PROGRAMMING, TELEPICTURES

"The biggest Hollywood stars turn to Lawrence to get on the best-dressed lists and now this is a chance for women everywhere to tap into his fashion genius. This is my top must-read book for 2014. And it's not just because I love Lawrence so much; it's because he is that good. He is a trendsetter, a style guru, and a great guy!"

—THERESA COFFINO, CO-EXECUTIVE PRODUCER, "EXTRA"

"Something magical happens in the fitting room when Lawrence is working with his clients. It's like the moment the caterpillar looks inside itself and realizes that it is a beautiful butterfly that can fly. I believe Lawrence possesses this ability, which has helped successfully transform women around the country, because his life's work comes from his own heart."

—PETER CHRISTMAN, VICE PRESIDENT OF STORES - WEST COAST, SALVATORE FERRAGAMO

"After many years of a style-less hair and a lackluster wardrobe, Lawrence helped me realize a new me. He knew the exact cut, color, and style my hair needed to look vibrant and healthy. And who knew that color and accessories would make a gal feel so glamorous? His patience and genuine care is why my makeover was a true success! He ignited the beauty that lies within, sparking a dormant romance between me and my husband. I will be eternally grateful to Mr. 'Fashion Guy' Lawrence Zarian!"

—SUZIE WILLIAMS: WIFE & MOTHER, NEW YORK, NY (MARRIED 11 YEARS WITH TWO BOYS)

THIS BOOK IS DEDICATED TO MY MOM, MY DAD &
MY BROTHERS, VINCENT & GREGORY.
THANK YOU FOR JUST LOVING ME... I LOVE YOU!

ACKNOWLEDGMENTS

First and foremost, I want to thank everyone who has allowed me to "make them over" during the past 15 years. Thank you for trusting me, my vision, and my super-talented team of experts. If it weren't for you, I wouldn't have this book. You will always have a wonderful place in my heart and each one of you has truly made me a better person! I'm humbled and grateful. Thank you.

When it comes to my career, I've been extremely blessed to have a few angels help me out along the way. First of all, I want to thank Nora Fraser for pointing me in the right direction. Mary Ellen DiPrisco for giving me my first shot on TV. Kym Douglas for introducing me to Woody Fraser. Woody Fraser for making me a family member on *Home & Family*. Laurie Gelman for orchestrating my first meeting with Michael at *Live! with Regis and Kathie Lee*. Michael Gelman for taking the meeting and giving me a shot—a shot that's lasted almost 15 years. Thank you, MG! Mariann Sabol for always throwing my name into the hat and for your honesty. Adora English for bringing me to the *KTLA Morning Show* so many years ago. Marcia Brandwynne for teaching how to *not* play the joke but letting the joke land organically. Lauren Berlly for bringing me on *Crook & Chase* and having everyone ask, "Where's Lawrence now?" Richard Ayoub and Steve Longo for introducing me to Lisa Gregorisch Dempsey at *Extra*. Lisa G for giving me a home at *Extra* for four awesome years. Michaela Pereira for loving me, my daddy and for teaching me the art of controlling the teleprompter. Matt Singerman for making me a part of the TV Guide family for four years. My TV wife, Daphne Brogdon. Brad Bessey for bringing me to *Entertainment Tonight*. And a special thanks to Janet Annino and Alex Duda for new adventures. I also want to thank my lawyer and friend, Scott Schwimer—you have stood by me and supported me for the past 15 years. I will always be grateful for you. I love you, Scotteeez!

I also want to thank Art Moore, Albert Bianchini, Anne Marie Williams-Grey, Debbie Dolins, Barbara Warren, Beth McCauley, Stephanie Schwartz, Ramey Warren, Sam Rubin, Leeza Gibbons, Kalina Rahal, Lynette Lewis, Tom Chasuk, Nancy Cruz, Robbie Ellis, Beverly Martin, Catherine Lippincott, Earl Nicholson, John Honsley, Brooke Perry, Kari Sagin, Andrea Capelli, Kelly Fordyce, Linda Bell Blue, Eliza Cost, Bonnie Tiegel, John Kosinksi, Michelle Orrego, Barry Poznick, Anne Lewis Roberts, Lisa Tatum-Roehrig, Cathy Palmerino-Levitan, Debra Duncan, Dr. Phil, Carla Pennington, Stephanie Granader, Neil Wolfe, Michelle Mekky, Berlinda Garnett, Chris Huston, Carla Koe, Tyra Martin, Nicole Perez-Kruger, Cheryl Maisel, Jeffrey Wilson, André Ortiz, Nikki Kemezis, Amy Bel Bruno, Kelly Williams, Ramey Warren, Lisa Tatum-Roehrig, Cathy Palmerino Levitan, Andrew Lear, Arnie Kleiner, Edd Adamko, Wendy McMahon, Cheryl Fair, Pam Chen, John Squatritto, Anne Vincent, Brigid Walsh, Cara Crowley, Amy Kule, Eliza Kazan, Linda Lee, Holly Thomas, Alison Kmiotex, and my gorgeous New York girls in MBA. Each one of you has had your hand in helping me and my career and I will forever be thankful.

Plus, a special thanks to all of the producers, directors, associate producers, PAs, camera men and women, grips, wardrobe, hair, makeup, and everyone else behind the scenes—you're the unsung heroes who work so hard in order to make it all look so easy. Thank you to some of the best shows on TV: the amazing staff at *Live with Kelly and Michael, Steve Harvey, Rachael Ray, The Doctors, Entertainment Tonight, Extra, On The Red Carpet, Home & Family, KTLA Morning Show, Good Morning Texas, WPIX Morning News, WGN Morning News,* and all the other shows that I'm fortunate to be a part of.

When it comes to writing a book, it does take a village and my village rocks. Thank you John Livesay for planting the seeds. Linda Lazar for helping me put my words on paper. JD Cargil for the strong push. Andrea McKinnon for opening the door at Bird Street Books. Jay McGraw for saying yes. Nancy

MacDonnell for the New York experience and all of your insightful contributions to the book. Carrie Genzel for helping me "work it out!" Bradford Rogne for your amazing eye. Michelle, Kate, Raf, and my John Varvatos family for making me look so good! Toni Pickett for always saying yes to yet "another photo shoot." Brooke Hagel for your patience and the gorgeous illustrations. Hagop Kalaidjian for your creative guidance. Brian Fox for going above and beyond and creating the perfect home for my words. Christine Schwab for showing up at exactly the right time and giving my book the final finesse. Thank you to Naomi Long for your keen eye and attention to detail. Plus, a special thanks to Josh Stein, Morgan Schutte, and the amazing Bird Street Books family. And finally, thank you Lisa Clark. Words will never describe the gratitude I have for you, your talent, and your time—thank you for loving this book just as much as I do. You are a gift and friend for life. I adore you. #Oscars

I also want to thank all of the talented people in my life—my friends who have contributed to this book—the experts, designers, artists, and celebrities. Actions speak louder than words, and the time you have given so freely speaks volumes. From the bottom of my heart, thank you.

Thank you to my friend and mentor, Regis Philbin for the beautiful foreword that you wrote. You have taught me so much, and our time together will always hold a special place in my heart. It doesn't get better than you! I'm blessed to call you my friend. I love you and Joy very much.

Thank you to my new friend, Steve Harvey, for writing such a wonderful afterword. You are a true inspiration and I love being a part of your TV family. The best part is that we have only just begun. Thank you, sir!

I want to thank Michael Gelman, Kelly Ripa, Michael Strahan, Rachael Ray, Lauren Conrad, DJ Petroro, Lisa Gregorisch Dempsey, Theresa Coffino, Brad Bessey, Alex Duda, Lauren Blincoe, Marie Griffin, Linda Lee, Peter Christman, Suzie Williams, and Lucy Long for your kind, generous, loving quotes supporting me and my book. I'm grateful.

I want to thank my friends who are truly my family. Each one of you continues to make my life better. You matter. Sheri Anderson-Thomas for giving me wings to fly. Lenora Eve for holding my hand when I was just starting my life all over again. Narine Arutunian, Josie Kinnear and her family, Michael Freeman, Lauren Berlly, Toni Pickett, Chris Dax, Crista Klayman, Susan Koziak, Melinda Martin, Dana Rosenberg, Victoria Levy, Theresa Coffino, Jennifer Dorogi, Bianca Dorso, Tony Maietta, Tracey Bregman, Laurie Gelman, Joe Lupariello, Joseph Ferraro, Mindy Stearns, Karen Samfillipo, Jasmin Mandatian, Nomi Bachar, Richard Reid, Randy Lopez, Evan Nisbet, Peter Christman and my Sunday night brothers, Craig Ramsay, Alice Vaghn, Jennifer Willis Karuletwa, Nina Avedissian, Andrea Jackson, Derek Opperman, Marcia Barnhart-Sharp, my GHS girls (you know who you are), Carole Jouroyan, Stephanie Edwards, Benjamin and Fabiana, Jim Caruso, Jennifer Abel, Jen Rade, Judith Light. And I can't forgot my two angels, Linda Manousos and my Patty Fox. You are all loved.

I also want to thank my entire family for all of their continued love and support. I'm sending some special love to my cousin Ava, and especially to Aunt Kima—thank you for watching everything I do. I love you.

Most importantly, I want to thank God for bringing so many talented, loving amazing and glorious people into my life. They have all made my life better. I'm humbled and blessed.

TABLE OF CONTENTS

LAWRENCE & REGIS PHILBIN

FOREWORD BY REGIS PHILBIN

I have been hosting talk shows for many years now; late night, afternoon, mornings. Right away, I learned that the morning show had a large female audience and what they loved were the makeovers we would do with ladies from all over the country. We called it the "Makeover" segment. Now, all we needed was someone who could handle all of this. And then, he was there! One look told us he could do it; there was no doubt about it. He had a great personality, a flair for fashion, and a way with the ladies that made them feel he was totally on their side. He was a good-looking guy who honestly cared about making these women look beautiful, feel so much better about themselves, and make their appearance on our show a day they would never forget. His name was Lawrence Zarian

He did all of it on his own. All we had to do was announce makeovers for our audience and ask the ladies to contact us if they were interested. Well, you know what happened: we were flooded with contestants. Sometimes we would make it an "ambush" makeover, where Lawrence would travel across America, get to the city or the town they lived in, get to their house, knock on the door, surprise them—sometimes shock them—and then explain that he was there to make them gorgeous. Sometimes he would have to sneak up to the house, ring the doorbell, and prepare to catch the woman as she fainted! A different makeover segment for each day of the week that required five ladies, and sometimes their husbands, boyfriends, kids, cousins—whoever wanted to join them were welcome—and that was just the beginning. Each makeover was a real production.

Lawrence orchestrated all of it with the help of the best experts in town. Just getting her hair done would take an entire day. The second day would be clothes, shoes, jewelry . . . you name it, she'd get it. This was the way it went for our five ladies. No one would be allowed to see them before they walked out on stage and joined the show. The husband, the boyfriend, the kids, even I didn't know what to expect. Lawrence would come out, give us a little background on the lady, show a picture of her, and then came the big reveal. I must tell you, it was magic when she walked out. The audience would go nuts! You had to be there to see the look on the husband's face; it was love all over again. It was something that made us proud of our show and proud of Lawrence, who did all of the above by himself. You simply cannot imagine what it took to put all this together, but he got it done for us, every time.

Over the years, Lawrence has become a friend of mine and my wife, Joy. She, of course, takes advantage of his talent. Sometimes they go into her closet to make big decisions on what goes, what stays, how this dress looks, what to wear with it, and what about the shoes? Honest to God, I don't know how he does it, but that's what he gets for becoming my friend.

Now, the question is—where does "Lawrence of Zarian" go from here? He's got it all . . . talent, looks, charm, and charisma.

It is time for him to shine even brighter. I can't wait to see it happen.

INTRODUCTION

The applause was almost deafening and the excitement was palpable. The audience couldn't believe their eyes . . .

Literally moments before, I had said, "Let's take a look at our girl before her life-changing transformation, and NOW let's take a look at the new Katherine!" She walked out, and it was as if everything had stopped. The audience was astounded, and most of all, thrilled for this deserving mother of three, a woman who had raised her children on her own for the past 15 years by holding down two jobs. Katherine's children wanted to express their love and gratitude for their mother in a grand way by nominating her with a "Thanks for Giving" makeover on her favorite morning talk show. Not only had Katherine received the VIP treatment by being pampered at the best spa in town, but in just 24 hours, I had taken this hard-working mother from simple and safe to stylish and oh-so-sexy! And the best part? She felt like a brand-new woman.

When I asked her how she was feeling, with tears welling in her eyes, she said, "I feel so pretty, Lawrence! Thank you for holding my hand; I couldn't have done this without you!" Needless to say, everyone was deeply moved by this mother's love and selfless devotion for her children and this amazing transformation. For the record, this mom looked FAB!

After the show, a glowing Katherine introduced me to her beautiful boys; we took photos, swapped emails, hugged one last time, and then I was off. It was Monday, and my week-long makeovers had just begun. One down, four to go! Quickly, I pulled myself together, changed clothes, and headed out into the lobby of the studio to meet my next makeover. Ten minutes had passed and still no one was there. Then suddenly, like a gust of wind, she rounded the corner, huffing and puffing as she entered the building. Words like "frantic," "crazed," and "disheveled" came to mind. She was clearly panicked.

Out of the thousands of applications submitted for our "Thanks for Giving" themed week, we chose five women ranging in ages and ethnicities, who had, in one way or another, touched us with their loving spirit and deep generosity. Back to my current makeover: windblown and frazzled, Victoria had just arrived. As she jammed her sunglasses into her purse, brushed her frizzy hair out of her eyes, and hiked up her baggy sweatpants, she started in with the apologies. "I'm so sorry, Lawrence! Oh my God, traffic was horrendous—my son's soccer practice went long . . . and then I . . ."

I gently put my hands on her shoulders and told her to just breathe. After a long moment, she let it all out. She was having "one of those days," and the thought of all this attention and time—being devoted to her—was just too much for her to handle. She was having a hard time calming down because her son had just started a new school and Victoria couldn't get her mind off of him. In the past six months, Victoria has completely uprooted their lives and moved out of the big city to a smaller town to protect her son from being bullied.

"My son is the most important thing to me and I just want to make sure that he's okay. I'll keep my phone on in case he calls . . . you know, if he gets scared or something." Her eyes were welling with tears. "He's such a good boy. I can't believe that he nominated me for this makeover. I just love him so much!"

A few moments passed, and I finally calmed her down. I told her that today was all about her and that we were on an adventure—a fashion adventure—to create a whole new look, from the inside out and from the ground up.

After a long moment, the words seeped in as she smiled, a smile that indicated she was ready to take this journey.

After a quick cab ride through the city, we arrived at our location, one of my favorite department stores. In order to assure Victoria that she was safe, I kept her hand in mine; it's such a big department store, it can be quite overwhelming and I didn't want to lose her. Working our way up through the store, we finally entered the executive offices and, once inside, I ushered her into the dressing room and asked her one simple but important question . . .

"What do you see when you look in that mirror?"

As soon as she met her own gaze in the reflection, I could tell she was about to lose it. She couldn't speak. She had no words.

This is probably the hardest part of my job—having a woman truly look at herself and accept who and what she sees in the mirror. I don't say anything, ever. I let the moment play itself out. It's painful. It's scary. It's a roller coaster of emotion. It's also a privilege for me to be there and hold someone's hand during such a vulnerable, honest moment.

After what seemed like an eternity, Victoria finally said, "Honestly? I see a woman who's given up. I see an old face staring back at me. Somewhere along the way I just stopped taking care of myself."

I squeezed her hand more firmly and said, "Honey, today you are the priority. Let me ask you this: When was the last time you went shopping and did something for yourself?"

She replied, "I can't even tell you; I don't even know what my sizes are anymore. I've gained weight, and I hate my body. I dye my hair myself; I wear the same sweats everywhere I go. I've given up on fashion, on clothes, on . . . myself," she said through heavy sighs.

I turned her toward me, wiped her tears away, and asked her, "Do you trust me?"

She said, "Yes, that's why I'm here. I trust you!"

"Then stop beating yourself up! What you do for your son is a testament to who you are and your actions speak volumes. Due to the fact that you take care of your son, it's my turn to take care of you for the rest of the day."

She rolled her eyes and said, "But look at me; is it possible? You know, to make me pretty again?"

"Sweetheart, it is possible. Let me assure you of that. You don't know it yet, but there is a stunning beauty inside of you, and I can't wait to help you show it to you and the world. You haven't given up; you've just been focusing on everything else that you love, except yourself. But right here, right now, in this very dressing room, we're going to find you and it is going to change everything." As I put my arms around her to give her a big hug, I asked, "I just need to know one thing. Are you ready?"

She nodded noncommittally, and I knew she wasn't sold yet. It had been so long since anyone had done anything for her, I knew that she had to see it to believe. I gave Victoria a few magazines, a cup of coffee, and told her to just relax and that her "fashion guy" would be back in a moment.

In a flash, I whisked myself out into the store to find some pieces to show her just how beautiful she was right now, in this moment. I chose a few items of clothing that would complement her size, such as form-fitting tank tops in neutral colors, a royal blue flyaway cardigan that works with the tanks, an assortment of floral, flirty dresses to show off her great legs and waistline, plus a pair of black pumps.

After my quick run through the store, I returned to the dressing room as Victoria was hanging up the phone with her son. "You sound good, honey. I love you and will call you later. Bye!"

"Hi, gorgeous, I'm back! How's your son? How are you?" She saw the stack of clothes in my arms and smiled.

"I'm good. He's good. We're good. Ahhhh!" I replied, "I'm glad. Now, are you ready to make it about you and play dress-up?" She giggled and said, "Yes. Yes. YES! Let the games begin!" Three dresses in, this courageous mother was beginning to see something beautiful in the mirror and she was loving what she saw. Big-time. (It continues to astound me how a little extra love and clothes that actually fit can make someone feel so good.) But we'll get back to her in a minute. I'd like to talk about you right now.

Does this scenario ring true for you? Have you given up on yourself? Do you feel like you're at the end of your wardrobe rope, unsure how to get your look back on track and hating everything in your closet?

Ahem. Well, it's nice to meet you. I'm Lawrence "LZ" Zarian, your own personal "Fashion Guy." Within the pages of this book, I have stuffed every style secret I've learned from my 20-year career of helping women of all shapes, sizes, and ages to create a look that is their own: unique and fabulous.

Excuse me while I brag for just a second — I'm only doing it because I want you to understand why you should take a leap of faith and trust me to help you. The reason talk shows call me to orchestrate their makeover segments is because I've honed my craft and I've learned what to do, because you women have told me what you're looking for. Sweetheart, I've listened and I'm still listening!

I know how to choose the right pieces to make you look and feel amazing. (In fact, later in this book, you'll see the the before-and-after photos of just a handful of the women I've had the extreme pleasure of making over.) Many of them still write me letters, showing me how they've maintained their new looks, how grateful they are for the help in uncovering their hidden potential, and for jumpstarting their lives.

Yes, I've been extremely fortunate and blessed to have assistance from the cream of the crop in the fashion, beauty, health and fitness industries and I don't want anything less for you. Period. So I went to the experts, my crazy-talented friends, and got their top tips and tricks and included those gems in this book, too. I've also included inspirational quotes from fashion icons and A-list celebs. (And you'll even find my cheeky hashtags scattered throughout the book, which will allow you to keep the stylish conversation going through your favorite social media outlets. #GetUrGlamOn) Everything you need is here! It's almost as good as having me and my entire dream team right there with you.

But let me be clear: you and I are about to embark upon a journey together. And by "journey," I'm not talking about just a trip to your local mall to get one new outfit. No, it's so much more. SO much more! In order for you to even wrap your head around what we're about to accomplish together, I need you to close your eyes, sit up straight, take a deep breath in through your nose, and exhale out through your mouth. As you exhale, imagine that all of your preconceived ideas about clothing, your appearance, and how you feel about yourself leave your body as you breathe it all out . . . and go. Pause. Do it again. It might feel so good that you'll want to do it just one more time.

Okay, now open your eyes and say out loud, "I'm ready." I can't hear you! Say it again. I'M READY. There we go; thank you. We've just taken the first step on our journey together! See? Not so bad, right? Painless.

This is going to be fun, but it can only be fun if you continue to let go of all the negativity you've associated with your looks and your wardrobe up to this point and embrace the positive. It's time to "try on" something different. Laugh instead of cry. Be daring. Get ready to act in brave, bold ways and for us to take some risks together. Remember, I'm here to guide you, and I will hold your hand every step of the way. I promise.

Let's go back for a moment into that dressing room with our friend Victoria, who was struggling. Now, pretend she's you. We've all been there. I've been there. As you read later on, I've spent years struggling with my own weight issues and self-image. It's a journey for all of us. I've spent most of my adult life with women just like you, down in the trenches, intently listening to their troubles, what they perceive as their personal figure flaws and all the reasons why they don't take the time to make themselves feel and look better. Countless women have come to me in the darkest hour of their lives—some of them have husbands who left them for younger women, others lost themselves as they put their families' needs above their own, still others suffered emotional abuse their entire lives or just always thought of themselves as the ugly duckling.

Whatever has happened to you, whatever obstacles or hardships life has thrown at you, those moments have made you who you are. In this book, I will help you say good-bye to the parts of your past that have been holding you back and say hello to a beautiful, confident, glorious new you so you can finally look in the mirror and love what you see.

By the time you finish this book, you're going to have all the tools necessary to re-create your look. You will learn just how easy, effortless, inexpensive, and truly joyful it can be to look your absolute best. More good news: you don't have to have a bank account the size of Ivanka Trump's in order to look stunning. If you're on a shoestring budget, you can still look amazing. Stop rolling your eyes; it's true! I'll show you.

My Ten Commandments celebrate women of all ages, shapes, and sizes. And yes, I'm talking to you, too . . . my gorgeous, voluptuous full-figured gals. The average American woman is a size 14 to 16, and due to the fact that I was the spokesperson for Lane Bryant for over seven years, I know exactly how to dress my curvy girls and celebrate those God-given curves.

There's also a chapter dedicated for your man. It breaks down the specific "must-haves" that every man needs for his wardrobe, plus some flirty tips for women to help get their man in step with style.

With my Ten Commandments, we're not only overhauling your wardrobe, we're giving your entire life a makeover, too. Beauty, after all, starts from within. Trust me, you've got all the pieces already; I'm just going to show you how to put your puzzle together. If you follow my Ten Commandments closely, you will be empowered to

- FALL IN LOVE WITH YOURSELF AND CELEBRATE WHO YOU ARE
- EMBRACE YOUR INDEPENDENCE
- LET GO OF THE PAST AND LIVE IN THE MOMENT
- REKINDLE AN OLD FLAME OR FIND THE PERFECT PARTNER
- ENHANCE YOUR MARRIAGE
- SCORE THAT JOB OR PROMOTION YOU'VE BEEN WAITING FOR

. . . and the list goes on and on. Why? Because confidence is sexy and powerful when you have a strong sense of self. By looking and feeling your best, the world will see a different you, and most importantly, YOU will see a different you.

Remember Victoria, the devoted single mother I mentioned earlier—the one who had made huge sacrifices to protect her son? Well, during our time together, she told me that she secretly wanted to look like one of those glamorous stars on the red carpet at a Hollywood premiere. As the saying goes, "Ask and you shall receive!" By the time I was finished with her, Victoria looked, in a word, incredible. With a little trust and by simply letting go, she could finally see that there was a stunning, bold, confident woman underneath all those extra layers.

She was a definite knockout as she practically floated across the stage. I had given her just the push she needed to see what an amazing, beautiful woman she had always been.

Okay, who's ready for a makeover? I know you are. Let's do it!

1 | THOU SHALT LOOK IN THE MIRROR AND LOVE WHAT YOU SEE

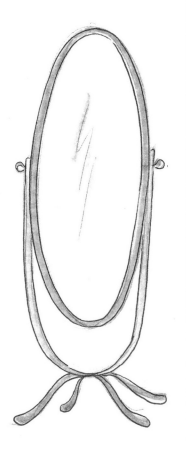

"THE BEAUTY OF A
WOMAN IS NOT IN THE
CLOTHES SHE WEARS,
THE FIGURE THAT SHE
CARRIES, OR THE WAY
SHE COMBS HER HAIR.
THE BEAUTY OF A WOMAN
IS SEEN IN HER EYES,
BECAUSE THAT IS THE
DOORWAY TO HER HEART,
THE PLACE WHERE LOVE
RESIDES. TRUE BEAUTY IN
A WOMAN IS REFLECTED
IN HER SOUL. IT'S THE
CARING THAT SHE
LOVINGLY GIVES, THE
PASSION THAT SHE
SHOWS, AND THE BEAUTY
OF A WOMAN ONLY
GROWS WITH
PASSING YEARS."

—AUDREY HEPBURN

■ POP QUIZ: Where does style begin? Okay, maybe it's not entirely fair to start with a question, but I want to make sure you're paying attention because my Ten Commandments will change your life if you will let them. Read them, absorb them, live them, and I guarantee you won't be the same person when you're done. It's a delicious prospect, isn't it? But to get to that point, you have to know where style begins. The answer is with you, babe. Read the title of this chapter again: Thou Shalt Look in the Mirror and Love What You See. Love. Not actively dislike, not make a face at, not tolerate. Love. Because that's what this commandment is all about: learning to love yourself.

THE LOOK OF LOVE

Now, I know we're right here at the beginning of the book, but I'm already going to ask you to do me a huge favor by stepping way outside of your comfort zone. But I believe if you can get the most challenging part out of the way first, all the rest will be smooth sailing. Deep breath. Here we go. #trust

STEP 1:   GO TO YOUR MIRROR.

STEP 2:   CLOSE YOUR EYES.

STEP 3:   TAKE A DEEP BREATH; EXHALE.

STEP 4:   WITH YOUR EYES CLOSED, TAKE OFF ALL YOUR CLOTHES
(AND THAT MEANS UNDERWEAR, TOO). HELLO! I CAN
SEE YOU. YES, YOU. DO IT. DO IT NOW!

STEP 5:   NOW THAT YOU'RE NUDE, TAKE ANOTHER DEEP BREATH.
HOLD, EXHALE, TAKE ANOTHER DEEP BREATH, AND THEN
LET OUT ALL THE AIR AND DO SOMETHING YOU MAY
HAVE BEEN AVOIDING FOR A LONG TIME . . . OPEN YOUR
EYES AND TAKE A GOOD, LONG LOOK AT YOURSELF.

STEP 6:   AAAAAHHH! CONGRATULATIONS; YOU'RE DOING IT!

STEP 7: TAKE ANOTHER DEEP BREATH; THROW BACK A DRINK IF YOU NEED TO AND TAKE A LONG, REALISTIC LOOK AT YOU. THIS IS THE YOU THAT GOD CREATED. WITH A SMILE ON YOUR FACE, SAY HELLO TO YOUR OTHER TEAM PLAYERS. HI, BOOBIES! HI, BELLY! HI . . . (INSERT CUTE LITTLE NAME FOR YOUR YOU-KNOW-WHAT).

Good job. Now that you made it through the first part (yes, there's more, so don't get dressed quite yet), take another deep breath and just breathe. Don't go anywhere; just look at you and take it all in. I'm serious; you can run, you can hide, but the facts are the facts, and unless you do this now, you'll keep running away from the truth—your honest, beautiful self.

We're not done yet, though. There are four sides to your pretty self. So, now it's time to turn to your left and look at your right side and take in your beauty from this view. Now, turn to the right so you can see the left side. And finally, it's time for the rear view. Turn around and, with either a hand mirror or just by turning your neck around, take another long look. With feeling! Yes, that's your butt. Hi, butt!

That's you. That's your butt, your belly, your breasts, your thighs—it's all you. Bare. Completely naked and beautiful, and only a lucky, chosen few get to see this lovely view.

Congratulations, gorgeous! You've accomplished a monumental moment, and you're definitely on your way. To where, you ask? To better style, that's where. You're probably wondering why I'm starting my book about fashion and style by first having you take off all your clothes. Yes, style is about what you wear. It's clothes, it's accessories, it's the whole package tied up in a shiny bow. That's what people see. But style and clothing aren't just what you wear; they're how you feel. And if you don't feel good, you're going to have a hard time looking good.

In the words of the ever-stylish Alicia Keys, "The most important thing to remember is that you can wear all the greatest clothes and all the greatest shoes, but you've got to have a good spirit on the inside. That's what's really going to make you look like you're ready to rock the world."

In order to feel good, first you have to be brutally brave, look at yourself honestly in the mirror, and accept where you are with your body. To do that, you have to first stare those "body issues" square in the face (so to speak) and confront their bare, naked truth—and you must accept them. That's what that little exercise in front of the mirror was about. See, I'm not crazy; I'm just forcing you to face you.

With everything we see on television and in magazines, we're overwhelmed with the perfect prototype of what we should look like; and it's disturbingly specific, right down to height, hair, and eye color. But that's not reality! I truly believe that God created us all individually. You can try 800 different things to change certain aspects of yourself, or you can decide to celebrate who you are at this moment in your life. Of course, that's not to say you're never going to change; we're always on a quest to improve ourselves, but you also have to love who you are right now, in this moment.

ONCE MORE, WITH FEELING

Look in the mirror again, and this time pay attention to your inner dialogue, the first place your eye goes, the first area you see that bothers you, and listen when you start saying to yourself, "Ugh, I hate my thighs, I hate those ugly stretch marks, I hate my saggy boobs and my extra belly rolls." Hear all that negativity? Come on, I can hear you beating yourself up from here!

Start the exercise over, but try something different for me. This time I want you to replace the word "hate" with "LOVE" and give it another shot. Repeat after me: "I LOVE my thighs, I LOVE my thighs, I LOVE my thighs." Rather than saying, "I will love my thighs after I diet myself down a couple sizes," I want you to love them as they are right now, this instant. Okay? Okay!

Now, obviously this exercise won't magically and instantaneously change how you view yourself, but if you keep it up, and make a real effort to catch yourself in those negative moments and tell yourself something positive instead, you can begin to make that shift. And that's exciting!

THE TRUTH BENEATH THE CLOTHES

From this point on, before we do any shopping—and yes, I promise we will get to shopping—you seriously have to make it a priority to get to a comfortable place with who you are and what your body looks like at this very moment. Just as a contractor must begin with assessing the foundation of a new house, you've got to start from naked before you start building your wardrobe. That's exactly what you just did by confronting and accepting your body beneath the clothes. Once again, I'm so proud of you—I'm hugging you in my mind right now.

When I do a makeover on a woman who hates her hips or wishes her stomach was more washboard than beach ball, and I tell her that she's better off wearing dark-rinse bootcut jeans rather than light-wash skinnies—well, let's just say it's like throwing a glass of water at a three-alarm fire. Sure, the intent is good, but you're not going to put out those flames. The bootcuts will enhance her natural shape, but they won't make her fall deeply in love with her body. Nothing on the outside will do that—it must come from within!

Women have taught me over the past 20 years that they wear their clothing to camouflage their emotions, and to me, that translates to their need to hide and not be seen. Maybe you tell yourself you're wearing baggy clothes all the time because you're more "comfortable" that way. But I believe you're wearing that oversized sweat suit or the stretched-out cardigan because you really just want to disappear and hide from the world under layers of excess.

Or maybe you go to the opposite extreme and pick out clothes that are way too tight and ultra-revealing. Going for the "sexpot" look, right? Well, maybe you're overcompensating for feelings of inadequacy and you truly believe that unless you show off your body, no one will notice you.

Style may sound superficial, but you really can't escape the fact that your style is a visible expression of who you are and what you're feeling about yourself. Your style tells your story to the world. What story are you telling about yourself? Think about that!

I know what I'm talking about here because all my life, I've struggled with my weight. In case you don't know this about me, I have an identical twin brother, Gregory. He truly is my best friend, but for most of my life, I was always the heavier twin and yo-yo dieting. Two years ago, my weight was at an all-time high, and I was emotionally eating everything in sight because I was suffering from the loss of one of my best friends and my father. The one thing I wasn't doing was taking care of myself. I hit rock bottom and I came to the realization, because of these devastating losses, that life is too short and I better stop being miserable and make some drastic changes. The first step was to get healthy. Two years have passed, and I've put a lot of work into turning things around and losing that weight (more on that in Chapter Three: Thou Shalt Be Healthy Inside and Out), but before any of that could happen, I, like you, stood in front of my mirror naked and had to accept myself as I was and love that person unconditionally.

"NOTHING MAKES A WOMAN MORE BEAUTIFUL THAN THE BELIEF THAT SHE IS BEAUTIFUL."
—SOPHIA LOREN

THE CONVERSATION INSIDE YOUR HEAD

Now, we're going to talk a lot about getting naked in this chapter, so let's return to that mirror moment, which really was just a moment, even if it felt like an eternity to you. Like lasers, your eyes probably zeroed in on the "no-like" zones, and everything else became just a blur. Chances are, your interior dialogue sounded something like this:

"Well, hello, tummy pooch. You're still there? Why do you have to stick out so far? Oh, and my old pal, muffin top, how you've grown! Is something wrong with this mirror? This is out of control. (Turn slightly to the side.) Holy ginormous butt—you're so much bigger than when I last saw you. OMG! Cottage cheese, anyone? Someone call Farmer John, I think one of his COWS escaped!"

Or something along those lines, right? I get it; it's human nature to focus on the negative. We all do it—I'm certainly guilty of it. We're hardwired that way. We have this built-in tape recorder that constantly reminds us of what we're not. Anytime I find myself having negative thoughts about myself, I immediately say, "STOP! That's not the truth." And then I force myself to throw those negative thoughts away. And if I need to, I say it again. There is not one ounce of truth in that negativity—it's all lies!

When you think about it, it's much easier to believe the bad about ourselves rather than the good. But my sincere hope is that with this book, we can work together to reprogram that dialogue, learn to notice and focus on all the good stuff about you (and there's a lot, whether you realize it yet or not), and cut out that self-deprecating script you've been telling yourself for years, maybe a lifetime. We—you and me—are going to CHANGE everything, and record some new inner dialogue.

WHY CHANGE?

You might be asking yourself, "Why is Lawrence so hell bent on changing how I feel about myself?" I'll tell you why! If you go around wearing ugly, unflattering clothes long enough, you just feel icky, and then you will eventually start to believe that you don't deserve any better. You'll just give up and live a life of accepting whatever is handed out to you because you don't deserve anything more than that. What kind of life is that?! Imagine me standing on a soapbox, with a big smile on my face, saying passionately, "I won't stand for it, and neither should you!"

On the other hand, if you put on something that was tailored just for you, something that flatters your shape and really defines your own personal style, you will begin to look at yourself differently. You will hold those shoulders back, you will give off a new, positive energy, and you will truly start to believe that you are worthy, you are beautiful, you are a star, and you deserve everything good that this world has to offer. All that from the right outfit? You betcha. It's a win-win.

GETTING NAKED ON THE INSIDE

We're brought up conditioned to always want more. But we have to remind ourselves that we have so much already. The way I stay grounded and in touch with this simple truth is through meditation, which, when you really look at it, is the mental and spiritual version of getting naked. I encourage you to try it; you will be so glad you did.

Try carving out 10 minutes at the start of your day and another 10 minutes right before you go to bed for meditation. Come on, you can do it. It's only 20 minutes and you need and deserve this. Go to a place in your home where you feel safe and won't be disturbed, and take stock of your life. Here's my routine: In the morning, I wake up, say my prayers, make coffee, and get myself situated, then I sit down in my safe space (in front of a bay window overlooking the hills) and I spend some time with God, as I understand God to be for me. Now, I'm not trying to get all religious on you here. I truly believe that everyone should have their own belief system, and that is a very personal choice for you and you alone. For me, God is loving, forgiving, kind, and gentle. I think of Him as the director of my life. If that imagery works for you, please feel free to use it. If not, substitute with your own. Make it as conceptual as you like. The point is, make it someone or something—male, female, whatever—that you feel comfortable with and loved by.

During my morning meditation, I mentally go through the day ahead. I have a checklist of what I need to get done, and I ask myself how I can accomplish these things authentically and with integrity. I make a plan. At night, I go through the day and take stock again. How did everything go? Did I lie? Was I deceitful? Could I have been a better person? And I list the things I'm grateful for. We spend so much time knocking ourselves that we forget how much we have, and that is no way to live! I am so grateful for so much: my health, my loving family, my precious nephews, my amazing and supportive friends, and my career. It's true; some days are better than others and even on my worst day, before I go to bed, I force myself to find a few things that I'm grateful for.

When I remind myself about these things, I feel blessed. I feel happy. I feel content. There is no better accessory than happiness, not even an all-expenses-paid, lifetime membership in the Manolo-of-the-Month club. (To the best of my knowledge, there's no such thing. But even if it does exist, I stand by my statement—and that's coming from someone who builds outfits from the shoe up.)

YOU ARE ENOUGH

No one, by the way, is immune to self-doubt. I definitely have my moments. You have no idea how many stunning models think of themselves as too fat, too short, too tall, too dark, too light, too ethnic. Even the most beautiful women in the world have self-image issues.

For me, the most profound example of this was Princess Diana. Her life was a fairytale. She married a prince and lived in a palace. She had two lovely little boys. She was gorgeous. She had a closet full of designer clothes and the glamorous lifestyle to match. Every woman wanted to be her. Then one day during an interview, she opened up and revealed that she was struggling with bulimia, exposing the pain, sadness, and self-doubt that so many other women have to deal with every day. What looked picture-perfect from the outside was anything but. This magnificent woman, who was beloved by the entire world, didn't like what she saw in the mirror. Is it any wonder the rest of us feel like we don't measure up?

"ONE DAY I DECIDED THAT I WAS BEAUTIFUL, AND SO I CARRIED OUT MY LIFE AS A BEAUTIFUL GIRL . . . IT DOESN'T HAVE ANYTHING TO DO WITH HOW THE WORLD PERCEIVES YOU. WHAT MATTERS IS WHAT YOU SEE."

— GABOUREY SIDIBE, OSCAR®-NOMINATED ACTRESS FOR THE FILM *PRECIOUS*

When young women tell me they want to look like their favorite stars on the red carpet, I tell them that anyone can have their hair and makeup done; I know that firsthand. I go through full hair and makeup before I appear on television and step into the persona of "lifestyle expert" on the air. They can make me look really good, but I still struggle, just like everyone else. At the end of the day, you're back where you started: naked. You strip off your clothes, remove your makeup and there you are again, naked as the day you were born. And that's the self you have to love. It's time to let go of the pain and accept yourself.

HOW TO PROPERLY MEASURE YOURSELF

WAIST: PULL THE TAPE MEASURE AROUND YOUR NATU-RAL WAIST, WHICH IS JUST ABOVE YOUR BELLY BUTTON, AND BELOW YOUR RIB CAGE. DON'T PULL IT TIGHT OR SUCK IN YOUR STOMACH—THE IDEA IS TO GET AN ACCURATE MEASUREMENT.

HIPS: START AT ONE HIP AND WRAP THE TAPE MEASURE AROUND YOUR BUTT AND THEN CIRCLE IT AROUND. AGAIN, DON'T PULL IT TOO TIGHT, BUT MAKE SURE THE TAPE IS PULLED ACROSS THE LARGEST PART OF YOUR BUTT—IT WILL BE MUCH EASIER TO DO THIS IF YOU'RE LOOKING IN A MIRROR.

INSEAM: START WITH THE TAPE MEASURE AT THE INNER PART OF YOUR THIGH AND PULL IT ALL THE WAY DOWN TO THE BOTTOM OF YOUR ANKLE. YOU MIGHT NEED A FRIEND TO HELP WITH THIS ONE. REMEMBER, THE PROPER INSEAM OF A PAIR OF PANTS YOU PUR-CHASE WILL DEPEND ON THE SHOES YOU'RE WEARING WITH THEM.

BUST: TAKE YOUR BUST MEASUREMENT WHEN YOU'RE WEARING A BRA WITHOUT PADDING TO GET THE MOST ACCURATE READ-ING. HOLD ONE END OF THE TAPE MEASURE ON THE FULLEST PART OF YOUR BREAST, WRAP IT AROUND YOUR BACK ALONG THE BRA STRAP, AND BRING IT ALL THE WAY AROUND. THIS WILL GIVE YOU AN IDEA OF YOUR BUST MEASUREMENT, BUT I ALWAYS RECOM-MEND THAT A BRA FITTING BE DONE PROFESSIONALLY BECAUSE IT IS SO WORTH IT TO GET THE BRA PERFECT; IT WILL HELP CREATE THE *PERFECT* LOOK.

Here's how I like to think of it: When we judge ourselves, berate ourselves, tell ourselves we aren't good enough, what we're really doing is saying to God (the ultimate fashion designer), "I don't like your work."

You are truly God's work of art! So, let's take a closer look at that work. Before I start a makeover, I always find out the basic facts about a person. Otherwise, it's a big guessing game. And why waste time guessing when we could be shopping? Right? Right!

So let's begin. First up, it's time for the facts. I want you to write down a few numbers (be honest!).

JUST THE FACTS, MA'AM

WEIGHT:	_____	DRESS SIZE:	_____
HEIGHT:	_____	JACKET SIZE:	_____
BUST:	_____	PANT SIZE:	_____
WAIST:	_____	BRA SIZE:	_____
HIPS:	_____	SHOE SIZE:	_____

If you truly don't know these details off the top of your head, then your very first mission is to find them out, pronto. Step on that scale, get out the tape measure, have someone help you take your measurements, and go to a department store for a bra fitting (don't be surprised if your size is not what you think—many women are wearing the wrong bra size!) and try on some clothes and shoes while you're there. Sizes can vary from designer to designer, but you need to start somewhere.

These are the raw materials of what you've got to work with. If you're 5'4", you're 5'4". You're never going to be 5'10". You can change your hair and eye color, at least temporarily, pretty easily, and with some dedication, patience, and effort you can change how much you weigh. But some things are just facts and we can't change them. Come to terms with who you are. And that, my dear, is someone pretty special and unique.

So let's document that. Write down three things that you tend to get compliments on—it can be your eyes, your fun personality, or your beautiful skin. I'm not talking about what you see, but what other people see. For me, people tend to compliment my height, my eyes, and my smile. Now it's your turn! Be honest; this exercise is for you, and it will start to change your inner dialogue.

YOUR TOP THREE COMPLIMENTS

ONE   _____

TWO   _____

THREE   _____

When you're doing this, don't be surprised if your mind tries to intrude and remind you of everything you don't like about yourself. Tell your mind to shut up! Give it a smack if need be. Try this: Imagine yourself dropping negative thoughts into the trash as you dance around the garbage can chanting, "It's not true, it's not true, it's not true." You don't have to dance or chant if you don't want to, but you get the picture: Those thoughts are going right into the garbage.

READING IS BELIEVING

Now, have a look at the three things you just wrote down and realize that they're true. I specified compliments because sometimes other people see us more clearly than we see ourselves. And I believe in the power of mass reinforcement. If three people tell you that your hair looks good, honey, your hair looks good. Believe it. You may get compliments about your nose, your hands, or your lips. Whatever they are, pay attention. It's so easy to believe in the worst about ourselves. So listen to and embrace the positive.

Next, I want you to email five friends. Choose the friends you trust the most and whose judgment you respect. Ask them to tell you what they love about you. I know that might sound crazy at first, but these are your friends who love and adore you, and they will be happy to tell you all the reasons why. You'd do it for them, right? Simply explain that you're on a journey to better yourself and your self-image, and that you're looking for a little positive reinforcement. I guarantee you will be amazed at what you get back.

HERE'S A SAMPLE LETTER THAT MIGHT HELP YOU GET STARTED

TO: _____

SUBJECT: _____

Dear _____,

I just started reading Lawrence Zarian's 10 Commandments for a Perfect Wardrobe, *and his mission is to help me change the way I see myself and celebrate what other people see. He believes that beauty comes from the inside out and that we must learn to embrace ourselves. One of his first steps in achieving this is to reach out to five important friends and ask them to tell me my three most beautiful attributes . . . because what I see and what you see are two different things. Because I love you and trust your judgment, please share with me the three things that you think are most beautiful about me. It could be anything—my sense of humor, my smile, my hair—it's up to you!*

Thank you for being in my life and sharing in this journey with me.

Love,

_____

Once your five friends have responded to your email, and you've thanked them, print out each one, find a quiet space, and read them to yourself slowly. Allow the words to wash over you and let yourself feel the positive reinforcement. Read them with a box of tissues, and just let your friends love you! On a personal note, I still have my emails and when I find myself feeling down, I pull them out and re-read them. It's a perfect pick-me-up. You can also keep them in your smartphone or jot them down on a Post-it and put them on your fridge or your bathroom mirror. #PositiveReinforcement

Am I saying that you should rely entirely on the way other people perceive you in order to feel good about yourself? No, no, a million times no! What I'm saying is that you need to open your eyes to how amazing you are to those close to you. They give you far more credit than you ever give yourself, I promise, and you need to hear that positive reinforcement from the people you love and who love you. You're going to use that information and build on it. You've gotten naked, and now it's time to wrap yourself up in positivity . . . that's a much better place to start.

There's one more thing I'm going to ask you to do. Yes, I can be bossy sometimes but only because I love you. So here it is: Take some pictures of yourself; these are your "before" photos. As you've seen with my makeovers, before we bring someone out for the big reveal, I remind the audience of what they used to look like before the transformation. Here are the basic rules of a good "before" photo.

- IT'S BETTER TO HAVE SOMEONE ELSE TAKE THEM, INSTEAD OF YOU TAKING THEM IN THE MIRROR. OR YOU CAN SET THE CAMERA ON SOMETHING AND SET THE TIMER. THE POINT IS, YOU NEED TO SEE YOURSELF FROM HEAD TO TOE.

- WEAR SOMETHING YOU TYPICALLY WEAR: YOUR "UNIFORM," YOUR GO-TO OUTFIT (NO MATTER HOW EMBARRASSED YOU MIGHT BE ABOUT IT).

- DO YOUR HAIR AND MAKEUP AS YOU USUALLY DO—EVEN IF THAT MEANS YOUR HAIR IS IN A KNOT ON THE TOP OF YOUR HEAD AND YOU'RE WEARING NOTHING BUT CHAPSTICK.

- MAKE SURE YOU'RE WELL LIT, WHETHER IT'S BY DAYLIGHT OR THE FLASH ON YOUR CAMERA.

- GET ONE SHOT FROM THE FRONT, ONE FROM EACH SIDE, AND ONE FROM THE BACK.

- DO A FULL-LENGTH SHOT, A THREE-QUARTERS SHOT, AND A HEADSHOT.

You are going to be so glad you have these. Keep them somewhere safe because you'll need them at the end of this book. And the only other thing I'm going to say about that right now is: prepare to be amazed.

CONTROL IS A WONDERFUL THING

By taking control of your style (with my help), you will be giving yourself the power to transform your life. There is nothing more positive than that, so watch out because other people are going to notice. You're going to be a walking, talking celebration of who you are because you will be dressing in a way that reflects that wonderful person inside.

Yes, I know, you might think I am a big cheese ball, but I really believe this. The greatest satisfaction I get from my job is helping people find the style that shows the world who they really are. You can look good. You deserve to look good. Believe that, and you'll be well on your way to fabulous.

Now let's get to work!

TOP FIVE TAKEAWAYS FROM LZ'S FIRST COMMANDMENT

ONE ACCEPT AND LOVE YOURSELF THE WAY YOU ARE.

TWO BE HONEST WITH YOURSELF ABOUT YOUR BODY. OWN IT. THIS IS WHO YOU ARE, AND THIS IS WHAT YOU HAVE. IT'S PERFECT, IT'S BEAUTIFUL.

THREE NO ONE IS IMMUNE TO SELF-DOUBT, BUT YOU HAVE THE CHOICE TO SEE YOURSELF DIFFERENTLY AND CHANGE YOUR INNER DIALOGUE.

FOUR WHEN OTHERS SAY NICE THINGS ABOUT YOU, LISTEN TO THEM, AND BELIEVE THEM.

FIVE TAKE "BEFORE" PHOTOS OF YOURSELF AND PUT THEM ASIDE FOR NOW; YOU'LL REFER TO THEM AGAIN ONCE YOU'VE WORKED YOUR WAY THROUGH THIS BOOK.

CONGRATULATIONS! COMMANDMENT ONE: ACCOMPLISHED.

2 | THOU SHALT COUTURE YOUR CLOSET

"I THINK WOMEN ARE REALIZING THAT MAYBE
THEY DON'T NEED A CLOSET FULL OF CLOTHES.
THEY JUST NEED THE RIGHT CLOTHES."

—MICHAEL KORS

Now that you've survived Chapter One and you've completely embraced and celebrated who you are—naked—let's venture into your bedroom. You can either get dressed or continue your nude celebration; it's up to you.

Hello, Chapter Two, my Second Commandment: Thou Shalt Couture Your Closet. No, I don't mean you have to run out and buy top designer labels and then, voila, you'll have the perfect closet. Not even close. In this chapter, I'm going to help you transform your closet into a stylish space of beauty and serenity.

Now, if your closet is anything like most people's, you've got some work to do (that might be a massive understatement). Let me see a show of hands for those whose closet exhibits the following characteristics: Every time you open the door you're showered with boxes, handbags, belts, and everything crammed on the top shelf. Or, a haphazard assortment of clothes for all seasons is jammed onto the rods or wire hangers. Maybe the floors are covered with mismatched shoes, dirty laundry, and discarded dry cleaner bags. Perhaps it even exudes a funky odor, or looks like World War III arrived! Not that I can see you or anything, but I sense a lot of raised hands out there.

The bottom line is that this is no way to live. If it's a mess, then you're probably—wait for it—a mess yourself (I say that with love) or working through something at this point in your life. The point is, you can't expect to paint a masterpiece if your canvas is full of holes and you've misplaced your paint set.

I know how easily this can happen, and it has happened to me many, many times. Life is in session and you're busy, plus your closet has doors on it, so you can just shut out the mess from the world and forget about it because who's going to see it anyway? Well, you are, that's who! I want you to love yourself enough to love your closet. It's true that no one sees the inside of your closet (except for maybe your husband or significant other), but that doesn't mean you can lower your standards. In order for you to look good, your closet must look good. There are no shortcuts.

When you open your closet doors, you should be excited and motivated to pick out your outfit but also feel a sense of calm. Your closet is where you get dressed and getting dressed should be enjoyable. You simply can't do it properly if it's a disaster in there and you have an anxiety attack every time you open the door. That's why I say that opening your closet door should make you feel both excited, because getting dressed is exciting, or it will be when I'm done with you, and calm, because you need to be calm to enjoy the excitement of getting dressed. This might all sound foreign to you, and yes, I can see you rolling your eyes, but I promise I will make it painless, easy, and fun.

Did you know it's estimated that women, on average, only wear 20 percent of the clothes in their closet? That's crazy, and such a waste of space and money! In my opinion, people just don't shop wisely. They don't know what they already have or what they actually need because their closet is a mess. They do what I have deemed "emotional shopping," which means buying something to fix an emotional issue, or because it's on sale, or because it's on trend even though they'll never wear it. Does this sound like you? Hi! It's okay. Never fear, your LZ is here, and I'm going to show you how to dissect your closet so that you utilize every piece of your wardrobe and make it truly work for you. #WardrobeWarrior

So, with no further ado, it's time to make over your closet.

YOUR CLOSET: THE PHYSICAL SPACE

COUTURE YOUR CLOSET STEP 1: CLEAN

The first thing you're going to do is empty your closet completely. I mean everything. Not just the clothes, but boxes, shoes, bags, hangers, rods, shelves, dirty laundry, yoga mats, dusty photo albums—all of it. But before you do that, you need to create a temporary space to house everything, and this can be anything from a corner in your bedroom to a living-room couch to the guest room. Be creative; you'll find the space. The reason for this is because, depending on the size of your closet and the work that needs to be done, this closet makeover might be time-consuming. And don't think of this as a job; think of this as creating a new space, a new beginning. So if you need to, take some breaks, get some food, check your Facebook and Instagram accounts (follow me on Instagram: @LawrenceZarian), whatever you can do to break it up.

Next, do a thorough cleaning. Dust, mop, vacuum, spray, wipe—put on some rubber gloves and give it the works. Depending on how OCD you are, this might be your favorite part of the process, or you might hate this, but either way, it has to be done. When I clean out my closet, I carve out some time and make it an event. I get my favorite drink, turn on my favorite music (music always makes everything better), and just start scrubbing.

Once it's all clean, stand back and give it a good look over. Does it need some help? I'm going to go out on a limb and guess the answer is a resounding yes. Okay, let's start with the big stuff. What's the lighting like in there? Nonexistent? It's amazing how many closets have no lights in them. This just does not work. If there's ever a place where you want to see things clearly, it's your closet. This is important for so many reasons! Think about it; life is hard enough—do you really need to waste time trying to figure out whether something is navy or black first thing in the morning? Really? Make it easy and come out of the darkness and into the light! It's nice out here, I promise. Get a light installed and you won't regret it. If you're on a budget, there are many affordable options to illuminate a small space that are easy to install. For example, I like tap lights that are only $6.99 at Bed, Bath and Beyond (www.bedbathandbeyond.com) or a clip-on light, such as the Fulcrum Multi-Flex LED Task Light that's only $11.99 at www.acehardware.com.

Next, are there any holes in the walls? Do you need to spackle and paint? If you're the DIY (do-it-yourself) type, head over to the hardware store for supplies. If not, find a handyman, or ask a neighbor or a family member. If you don't have the extra money, post something on Facebook or ask a friend for help. I know it might seem silly to put so much TLC into such a small space in your home, but this isn't just about your closet; this is about YOU, and you are important. You deserve better than chipped walls and a dreary color. A little spackle and a vibrant paint color will work wonders. Get creative and have a little fun with the color you choose. Here are some of my personal favorites, but go with what will create the right mood for you:

- EGGSHELL WHITE— CLASSIC AND CLEAN
- PALE LAVENDER—THE MOST SOOTHING COLOR OUT THERE
- PEARL GRAY—ELEGANT AND ALWAYS APPROPRIATE

COUTURE YOUR CLOSET STEP 2: DECORATE

Yes, decorate. Who decorates a closet, you ask? Um. I do, and I think you should, too. I'm not talking about putting up drapes and shopping for cute accent pillows. You just need to make it a warm space, one that reflects your personality and style. The Duchess of Cambridge, one of the most stylish ladies to ever rock a couture gown, had her boudoir painted to look like there was lingerie spilling out of all the drawers. Obviously she had a royal-size budget and I'm not suggesting you do that, but you get the idea: Make the space your own.

You've started that by choosing a flattering paint color. Now let's talk about structure: the rods, drawers, and shelves that are going to make up the backbone of your storage system. There are some fabulous companies who specialize in closet organization, such as the Great American Closet Company and California Closets, or you can go online and find one in your area that works with your budget. They'll help you assess the space you've got to work with, make helpful suggestions on how to maximize it, and then come in and build your personalized dream closet.

If you'd rather get up-close and personal with closet organization (or one that's more along the lines of what your budget allows), there are plenty of options for you at prices for every budget. I like the following:

IKEA (WWW.IKEA.COM): Like everything IKEA does, their closet solutions are well designed, well thought out, and just generally a brilliant way to save money. (#LoveThat) I like the ALGOT system of shelves, hanging rods, and drawers, which can be slotted into any space you have and complemented with IKEA's huge range of bins and baskets. If you want to build a stand-alone wardrobe, the PAX ones are fantastic and completely customizable. If you don't live near an IKEA, you can order online. And in many areas, they even offer installation services.

ELFA (WWW.CONTAINERSTORE.COM): elfa is the Container Store's version of the custom closet, and I've got to say, it's pretty fab. You can shop by the component or give your specs to an elfa specialist and have them design the whole thing for you. It can all be done online, too. (Here's an LZ tip: If you're wanting a closet makeover, ask your friends and family to give you Container Store gift cards for your birthday, holidays, or just because they love you.)

TARGET (WWW.TARGET.COM): Target is a treasure trove of colorful options for organizing your closet, including some clever ways to store jewelry, scarves, and shoes. I love the clear acrylic drawer inserts for keeping your intimates and other small items under control, and they allow you to see everything.

WAL-MART (WWW.WALMART.COM): Wal-Mart stocks Rubbermaid's line of closet organizers, which get the job done at minimal cost. Also a great place to pick up hangers and those hanging sweater shelves.

COUTURE YOUR CLOSET STEP 3: SCENT

Your closet is a multisensory experience, so let's not ignore how it smells. Whether you choose to spray or sachet, make sure it's a scent you like and one that doesn't fight with your favorite perfumes. A couple of classics that I use are lavender and cedar.

LAVENDER: Herbal and relaxing, with spicy undertones, and helps chase away moths. And lavender has traditionally been praised for its calming and soothing qualities. You can buy lavender in bunches, strip it from the stems and put it in little sheer jewelry bags, and hang them on your hangers. Just squeeze the bags every once in a while to release the oils and fragrance.

CEDAR: Fresh, with a woodsy scent, and excellent at repelling moths.

COUTURE YOUR CLOSET STEP 4: SEASONAL INSPIRATION BOARD

Inspiration is key when you're getting dressed. So consider putting together a seasonal "mood board" of trends and inspirations and hanging it inside or near your closet. These exist in every designer's studio for a reason—they synthesize everything you want to say in one easy-to-read place. This doesn't need to be fancy or complicated.

Here's what you do: Thumb through your favorite fashion magazines and tear out the pages you like for style inspiration and pin them to a corkboard. You could even take it one step further with color swatches, quotes, or whatever else strikes your fancy.

COUTURE YOUR CLOSET STEP 5: ORGANIZE

You now have a fresh, clean, and empty space. Next up: Let's get it organized. To some extent, how you organize your space is going to depend on your lifestyle and preferences. If you wear a lot of jeans and sweaters, you're going to need more shelf space. If your work attire requires lots of suits, you'll need more rod space. If you attend a lot of evening events, you're going to need hanging space for full-length gowns. The important thing is to create your space to suit your wardrobe.

Here are some basic guidelines. These are just suggestions and can be somewhat of an investment, but if it's within your budget, it's worth it to invest in some hangers that you'll have forever. Hanging your clothing properly will definitely extend the life span of your garment. If you are good to your clothing, it will be good to you. Note: You can find good quality wooden hangers at your favorite department store or online. Check out the ones that Bed, Bath and Beyond has to offer: www.bedbathandbeyond.com.

SUITS: Suits need contoured wooden hangers that support their shoulders and that have a crossbar for hanging a pair of trousers over or clipping a skirt to. One suit per hanger!

DRESSES: Hang dresses on either contoured wooden hangers or substantial plastic ones. Spaghetti-strap and strapless dresses should be hung from loops or ribbons stitched to the inside of the dress; if they're not there, sew 'em in. It will take two minutes and extend the life of your dress. Organize by length and color so you can quickly spot what you need. (Note: Dresses that are cut on the bias should be folded over a hanger. Otherwise, they'll stretch out of shape. PS: A bias cut means that instead of cutting the garment so that the weave of the fabric is straight up and down, it's cut diagonally.)

PANTS: I like pants hangers (they're shaped like a regular hanger but with an open side for easy access), but regular hangers, provided the crossbar is thick enough, work just fine. I also like the individual pants hangers, designed just for pants. It's all about choices, choices, choices.

SKIRTS: Hang your skirts on skirt hangers. If you're pressed for space, use a hanger that staggers four or five skirts altogether. Skirts that are cut on the bias should be folded over a hanger.

CLOTH JACKETS AND COATS: Store as you would a suit jacket, on a contoured wooden or heavy-duty plastic hanger.

LEATHER JACKETS AND COATS: Hang as you would a cloth jacket or coat and make sure the closet is well ventilated. Never put leather in a plastic dry-cleaning bag—it will dry the leather out.

SWEATERS: Never hang your sweaters. Instead, fold and stack them. Tuck a few cedar chips or other moth deterrents in with your sweaters. Do not stuff too many sweaters into too small a space or they'll wrinkle. When it comes to expensive items like cashmere sweaters, I suggest storing them in Ziploc baggies to keep the shape and prevent moths.

JEANS: Fold and stack by color.

LINGERIE: Stack bras by the cup and store in a drawer—do not overcrowd. Panties, camisoles, and slips get folded and stacked. Scatter a sachet or

two in there. Or, better yet, spray your perfume on tissue papers and place them in the bottom of the drawer.

JEWELRY: When it comes to jewelry, depending on your space, you have many options. Personally, I always suggest clear hanging jewelry bags that not only save space, but show you exactly what you have. My favorite is called The Little Black Dress Hanging Jewelry Organizer by Umbra that I found at www.containerstore.com for only $19.99. (It houses everything from earrings to bracelets, necklaces and rings.)

SCARVES: You shouldn't shove your scarves in a drawer or in a container because they'll wrinkle. Let them hang out and breathe. For $9.99, you can get the Axis Scarf Holder that will hold up to 18 scarves, shawls, and kerchiefs at www.amazon.com.

HATS: Once again, hat storage depends on how much space you have. You can either stack them on top of each other to help keep their shape, or you can hang them on your wall with an adhesive hook that won't damage your wall, such as the Command brand large hooks that you can find at www.command.com.

TOOLS OF THE TRADE:

INGENIOUS CLOSET GADGETS

THESE ACCESSORIES WILL SOLVE SOME OF YOUR MOST DIFFICULT
CLOTHING-STORAGE ISSUES.

BAROQUE RUBBER HANGER
FROM UNITREX, APPROXIMATELY $16 FOR 6
WWW.AMAZON.COM

THESE CLEVER HANGERS HAVE CURVY FRAMES THAT WILL KEEP
SPAGHETTI-STRAP TOPS AND DRESSES FROM SLIDING TO THE FLOOR.

METAL SHOE STAX
FROM BOOTTIQUE, APPROXIMATELY $20 FOR 6
WWW.BOOTTIQUE.COM

YOU CAN DOUBLE YOUR SHOE-STORAGE SPACE WITH THIS HANDY
GADGET, WHICH LETS YOU STACK PAIRS OF SHOES.

BOOT ORGANIZER
FROM REAL SIMPLE, APPROXIMATELY $30
WWW.BEDBATHANDBEYOND.COM

THIS INGENIOUS BOOT RACK HANGS OVER YOUR CLOSET DOOR
AND HOLDS FOUR PAIRS OF KNEE-HIGH BOOTS.

PLIIO BY THE INSERTS
APPROXIMATELY $25 FOR 16
WWW.QVC.COM

FOLD YOUR T-SHIRTS AND TANKS AS NEATLY AS THEY DO AT THE
STORE WITH THESE REUSABLE INSERTS.

Now, when coordinating your bins and various other storage boxes, choose a color scheme and style and stick with it. It doesn't need to be fancy, but when everything matches, it will vastly improve your experience when you open that closet door every day. All I'm suggesting is an afternoon at your local 99¢ Only Store, Container Store, IKEA, or Target. They've got a gazillion options, any one of which will be many, many times better than a messy hodgepodge of ugly boxes, bins, and baskets. #BudgetFriendly

About your hangers. I just can't hold out any longer. Stop with the wire hangers, already! Not to get all *Mommie Dearest* on you, but is that any way to treat your clothes? Wire hangers look perfect with a marshmallow hanging off the end of them over a campfire, but other than that, no way. Just because the dry cleaner gives you one with every garment you have cleaned doesn't mean you need to give that thing a home. Gather 'em up, return them to your local dry cleaner, and get yourself something better.

I'm not picking on wire hangers just because they're ugly, by the way (well, maybe a little). A hanger's whole purpose in life is to provide support for the clothing that's put on it. Wire is just not up to the job. Heavier plastic is fine for blouses and dresses, but anything tailored or bulkier, like a jacket or coat, needs a contoured wooden hanger that can support its weight without buckling under the pressure. That way, when you put something on, the shoulders hang properly instead of looking like they've been dislocated in some weird fashion accident.

See? There's method to my madness. Plus, if all of your hangers match, your closet will more likely give off that "well-edited boutique" look rather than that "super-sloppy garage sale" look. And that's motivational when you're getting dressed and when you're putting things away. Suddenly, it won't feel like such a chore to do laundry or put the dry cleaning away. It will all be part of maintaining your lovely new closet space.

Speaking of laundry, how's your laundry hamper situation? If you don't have a good one, invest in one. My preference is the kind with the separate compartments for darks, lights, and delicates. When something needs to be washed, drop it in there instead of on the floor, under your bed, or wherever else it may end up. Get another hamper for dry cleaning and check it every couple of weeks. It makes much more sense to drop off dry cleaning in bulk than to run down there every few days. And lots of dry cleaners offer coupons for multiple items and many accept coupons from other dry cleaners, just like car washes.

And no matter what, you must, I repeat, must get a full-length mirror (you can get one for under $20, and considering the fact that you're priceless, what's $20?); and do not walk out the door without looking into it. NO EXCEPTIONS! Here's another LZ tip: Have a handheld mirror near the full-length mirror so you can check your backside too. There's nothing worse than looking good when you walk in, and not-so-good when you walk out. It's all about the 360 degree view, babe. #HelloGorgeous

Okay, we're clean, we're tidy, and we're ready to have some fun.

YOUR CLOSET: THE CONTENTS

Now that you've made your closet space as beautiful as you can, let's talk about what goes inside. Remember that big pile of clothes we made earlier? We're going to get started on those clothes now. You've probably heard about how we use only a fraction of our brains, right? The same is true of our wardrobes. It is very likely there is a portion of your wardrobe that's doing nothing but taking up precious real estate in your closet. Plus, another part of your wardrobe is just begging to be worn. That's right; there are some perfectly amazing garments in there, but you've gotten so used to pushing past them

or not even seeing them that you've forgotten they exist. But don't fret; it's time for a wardrobe reconciliation, because I'm going to help you rediscover these items that are in there just dying for some attention.

The glorious Diane von Furstenberg, the inventor of the jersey wrap dress, which no closet is complete without, once admitted, "There are so many things I've bought through the years, worn once, and realized they are just not 'me.' Personal style is accepting who you are!" If it can happen to DVF, it can happen to you.

So please have an open mind here and trust me. I'm with you every step of the way to give you guidance, ideas, and my trademark charm (wink), but this is going to call for something a little more up close and personal. So I want you to invite your closest and most honest friend over to your place, make a few cocktails (or mocktails, whatever works!), set out a few snacks, and create your own mini closet fashion show. This is also known as channeling your inner supermodel (or your inner Carrie Bradshaw, whichever suits you), turning on some music, and getting a little cray cray with your clothes. #supermodel

Theoretically, I suppose you could do this on your own, but drinking by yourself, even if it's of the nonalcoholic variety, is no fun at all . . . but more importantly, even with the best of intentions, you're going to overlook possibilities that someone who's less intimate with your closet will spot right away. So brace yourself and get ready. Hey, you've already looked at yourself naked, so now it's time to take another step in a new direction and take a serious look at your wardrobe.

Let's say you have an old, faded college sweatshirt that you like to wear to run errands in. To you, it's casual and fun and reminds you of your youth. To everyone else, it's seen better days and makes you look like an aging sorority girl (not your best look). The best part about an honest friend is that they'll point that out to you; they'll also celebrate other pieces in your wardrobe that they've never seen, and say things like, "I've never seen you in those pants; they make your ass look amazing!"

You've set the stage; now it's time to try everything on. Mix, match, and try out new combinations. Be fearless. You don't have to wear any of these looks on the street; this is just you and a close friend in the privacy of your own home. You're going to see some old favorites in a whole new light and discover buried treasures. And you're also going to do a lot of weeding out because, kids, I promise you, there is a whole lot of uselessness going on in your wardrobe—this is true for anyone who doesn't do this often.

Let's start with the two most important rules of wardrobe management. Attention, please, attention! Listen up, your Fashion Guy is making a point.

WARDROBE MANAGEMENT 101

1. YOU SHOULDN'T OWN ANY ITEMS OF CLOTHING THAT YOU DON'T LOVE. Obviously, this is relative. You will not love a pair of socks with the same passion that you have for the perfect cashmere sweater. But the principle remains the same: If the socks don't speak to you, if they're not the exact color and texture you want, why are they in your life? Pass them on.

2. EVERY ITEM IN YOUR WARDROBE MUST PULL ITS WEIGHT. That means that unless you're wearing something regularly, it needs to go. If it goes with nothing else in your closet, it needs to hit the donation sack. If it was a great bargain but is three sizes too small, toss it or start your bag for Goodwill or your favorite charity. If your mother gave it to you but you can't stand the color, say buh-bye. If it's got a stain that has resisted numerous dry cleaning attempts, it's done. You get the idea.

As you apply these rules, and as you go through the pile of stuff, you may find that you discard more than you keep. Do not panic. This is perfectly normal. You may end up with a lot less stuff hanging in your closet, but trust me; it will be for the best. The clothes that make the cut will be the pieces that are flattering on you and, most importantly, make you feel good. (In case you haven't been paying attention, I'm your walking, talking, fashionable Hallmark card, and I just want you to love yourself. I'll keep interjecting these hugs and kisses throughout the book.)

"SEXY ISN'T THE CLOTHES YOU WEAR, IT'S THE WAY YOU WEAR THEM.
SEXY IS HOW YOU OWN YOUR OWN POWER."
—JUSTIN TIMBERLAKE

IMPORTANT: Not everything is worthy of being donated to the needy. Seriously, if it's worn out and beyond all repair, nobody wants it. I'm talking about shirts with permanent sweat stains under the arms, sweaters that are pilled and moth-eaten, suits that have been dry-cleaned so many times they give off a glare—pile all of it into a black trash bag and throw it away or recycle it.

Now that you've gotten rid of the damaged goods (pun intended), we'll turn our attention to everything that wasn't voted off "Closet Island." But before you officially put something back into your wardrobe, ask yourself the following questions:

1. HAVE I WORN IT IN THE PAST THREE YEARS?
2. DO I FEEL CONFIDENT EVERY TIME I PUT IT ON?
3. DOES THIS FLATTER MY FIGURE?
4. DO I FEEL SEXY WHEN I WEAR IT?
5. IS THIS GARMENT STILL ON TREND OR CLASSIC ENOUGH TO KEEP?

If you've answered "no" to three or more of these, it's time to say adios and send it packing. Consider taking it to a consignment shop or eBaying it and making some extra cash to buy new things. If you paid so much for it that you're having trouble letting it go, look at it this way: You've already paid for it, and now you're paying for it psychically every day by having it in your closet, taunting you and taking up valuable space. Donate it, give it to a friend, or get rid of it. If you haven't worn it because it won't fit until you lose that last five pounds, do the same. When you lose the weight, you have my permission to go out and celebrate by getting some new things. In the meantime, having clothes in your wardrobe that don't fit is reminding you what you're not and can just make you feel bad.

Remember, you can't go back and you don't know the future, so choose to live in the moment and always wear clothes that fit. Sometimes it's hard to let go of something for sentimental reasons, even if you know you're never going to wear it again. I'm not telling you to toss your wedding dress but I do think that these garments need to be separated from your regular clothes. It's distracting to be looking for something to wear to a big meeting and be confronted with a special occasion dress from way back when.

Wedding dresses and other valuable items should be dry-cleaned, folded, and stored in acid-free tissue paper. For everything else that falls into this category, you can keep no more than what can be stored in one garment bag. Consider it tough love; if you kept everything you felt sentimental about, you would definitely be drowning in clothes.

If you're having separation anxiety just thinking about getting rid of old clothes, then do it in stages. First, put everything you want to get rid of in a box or bag and keep it close to your closet. After a week, put the bag or box next to your front door. After another week, take it to Goodwill, Out of the Closet, or whatever charity you like. You won't even notice it's gone, I promise.

EVEN GOODWILL DOESN'T WANT IT IF . . .

. . . THE ARMPITS ARE SUPER STAINED.

IT SMELLS BAD.

. . . MOTHS HAVE BEEN FEASTING ON IT.

. . . YOUR DOG OR CAT HAS BEEN USING IT AS A CHEW TOY.

. . . IT'S UNDERWEAR AND YOU'VE WORN IT (IN A WORD . . . YUCK!).

You're now left with a smaller but significantly more useful wardrobe. I know, change is hard, but this is all for the best. And look at it this way, too: now you've got room for new clothes! YAY!

So, here's the big question: Just what should you do with all that extra space? Oh, I'm so glad you asked because I happen to have strong opinions on what makes the perfect wardrobe.

LZ'S WARDROBE FUNDAMENTALS

HERE'S WHAT I CONSIDER THE BASICS OF A GREAT WARDROBE. NOTE: I'M NOT SAYING YOU HAVE TO GO OUT AND BUY ALL OF THESE PIECES; THAT WOULD COST A LOT, AND I ALWAYS WANT TO BE RESPECTFUL OF YOUR BUDGET. BUT PEOPLE ASK ME ALL THE TIME ABOUT THE MUST-HAVES FOR A PERFECT WARDROBE, SO HERE'S THE LIST. BUY WHAT YOU CAN, WHEN YOU CAN.

A LITTLE BLACK DRESS IN A STYLE THAT SUITS YOU.

A TWO-PIECE PANTS SUIT IN BLACK, NAVY, GRAY, OR BROWN.

A BLACK PENCIL OR STREAMLINED SKIRT (AND FOR MY FULLER-FIGURED GALS, YOU CAN DEFINITELY FIND LONGER BLACK SKIRTS THAT ARE MADE JUST FOR YOU AND YOUR SEXY SIZE).

THREE PAIRS OF JEANS—ONE THAT YOU CAN WEAR TO WORK (IF YOUR WORKPLACE ALLOWS), ONE HEMMED FOR HEELS, AND ONE HEMMED FOR FLATS. IF YOUR BUDGET ALLOWS, WHEN YOU FIND A GREAT PAIR OF JEANS THAT FIT, BUY SEVERAL PAIRS SO YOU HAVE BACKUPS.

CLASSIC FLAT-FRONT PANTS IN KHAKI, BLACK, NAVY, GRAY, OR BROWN.

A WHITE BUTTON-DOWN SHIRT—FYI, NO ONE DOES THESE BETTER THAN BROOKS BROTHERS (WWW.BROOKSBROTHERS.COM). IF THEY'RE GOOD ENOUGH FOR MADONNA AND LADY GAGA, THEY'RE GOOD ENOUGH FOR YOU. ANOTHER OPTION IS J. CREW: WWW.JCREW.COM.

A SELECTION OF BLOUSES IN AN ASSORTMENT OF VIBRANT COLORS.

- TWINSETS IN CREAM, BLACK, RED, OR YOUR FAVORITE COLOR.

- AN ASSORTMENT OF TANK TOPS AND TEES IN NEUTRAL COLORS.

- A TURTLENECK SWEATER IN BLACK, CREAM, OR A PRIMARY COLOR.

- A PATTERNED JERSEY WRAP DRESS.

- A BLACK AND NAVY BLAZER.

- A CLASSIC TAN TRENCH COAT THAT HITS BELOW THE KNEE.

- A WINTER COAT IN A DARKER COLOR LIKE BLACK, NAVY, GRAY, OR RICH, CHOCOLATE BROWN.

- A LEATHER BLAZER OR MOTORCYCLE JACKET (DON'T FORGET THE POWER OF "PLEATHER.")

- UNDERWEAR AND FOUNDATION GARMENTS. THE BARE (NO PUN INTENDED) MINIMUM IS 2 WORKOUT BRAS, 3 T-SHIRT BRAS, 2 CONVERTIBLE BRAS, 10 PAIRS OF PANTIES, AND 1 TO 2 OF WHATEVER SHAPEWEAR YOU NEED.

- TWO BATHING SUITS IN WHATEVER STYLE YOU LIKE BEST, AND COVER-UPS. (LZ FUN FACT: GO TO YOUR GUY'S SIDE OF THE CLOSET AND GRAB ONE OF HIS SOLID COLOR OR STRIPED DRESS SHIRTS AND USE IT AS A SEXY COVER UP. #CHIC)

You should be able to create four or five different "looks" with every piece on this list. For example, you could wear the white button-down with the pencil skirt, with the suit, with the khakis, with the jeans, or as a cover-up over your bathing suit. Switch out your accessories and these basic pieces will take you anywhere.

BUDGETS: A REALITY CHECK

Again, please don't think I'm asking you to go out and blow your budget on a new wardrobe. Accepting yourself means accepting everything about yourself, including your budget. If you can't afford designer clothing, be honest with yourself and just don't buy it. You're setting yourself up for the headache of debt. Work with what you have. If you don't have a white button-down shirt but you have a pink one or a blue one, wear that. If your pants are brown instead of black, that's fab. Another LZ tip: People remember the tops you wear more than the bottoms, so classic styles and colors on the bottom can be worn several times in a week. And solid color tops have more staying power than prints because prints are memorable. You can't wear a print shirt twice in one week, but you can wear a solid white, a soft blue, or a petal pink more than once if you add a vest, cardigan, or scarf.

When I find something I want, each week I put a little money aside and save for it. I'll make a temporary sacrifice in one area of my life until I have enough money to buy what I've been obsessing about. That might mean cutting out movie nights, extra dinners out, or just my iced cappuccino in the morning. As you continue to build your wardrobe, and you've saved some extra cash, here are some luxe pieces to consider:

- A FUN, FANCY DRESS
- A GOOD CASHMERE SWEATER
- A DRESSY COAT FOR EVENING
- A DESIGNER SILK BLOUSE IN YOUR FAVORITE COLOR
- A TOP DESIGNER PURSE
- A SEXY PAIR OF HIGH-END SHOES

If buying all these pieces is a luxury you can't afford, there are ways to assemble a good, basic wardrobe that won't break the bank. One method I like that doesn't cost a dime is to shop in a girlfriend's closet—with clothes of a similar size. Once you've weeded out your closet, invite her over to go through some of your "treasures" too. The saying is true—what you might think is trash will be a treasure to someone else, and vice versa. You'll each get new things, you'll get to spend some time together, and you won't have racked up any credit card guilt.

TAKING CARE OF YOUR WARDROBE

If there's one thing that makes me insane—okay, besides ugly shoes—it's sloppiness. Regardless of whether an outfit is put together nicely or not, when I see people with missing buttons or stains, I have to restrain myself from removing the offending pieces from their bodies. (If you spot me out in public and I'm sitting on my hands with a pained expression on my face, you'll know why.)

The essence of chic is good grooming, and no well-groomed person walks around looking messy. Why put all the effort into assembling and storing your wardrobe if you're not going to take care of it? Trust me when I say that nothing ruins an outfit like a sagging hem or a top that should have gone to the dry cleaners three wears ago. If you even have to ask yourself whether something needs to be cleaned, then the answer is, drumroll, please . . . yes! Love yourself enough to wear clean clothes.

When something needs to be washed, wash it or take it to the dry cleaner. When it needs a repair, fix it yourself or bring it to a tailor. If you don't have a tailor, your dry cleaner will do minor repairs at half the price. The point is, keep on top of these things or you'll have nothing to wear but clothes that are in a state of semi-disrepair—or, as I sometimes think of it, semi-despair.

WASHING VS. DRY CLEANING

Some people dry-clean everything. I understand the appeal of this. It's incredibly convenient, and I've been known to do this for the sake of convenience myself. But this approach doesn't do your clothes any favors. If you dry-clean constantly, fabrics are going to get limp and lifeless and eventually take on that telltale shine that comes from your dry cleaner being heavy-handed with the industrial iron.

Now, don't get me wrong—I fully believe that dry cleaning is one of the wonders of modern life. But as with all things, moderation is key. So if you're a dry cleaning addict, I hope you're sitting down when I deliver this little news flash: not everything needs to be dry-cleaned every single time you wear it. #breathe

Here is my three-step garment check to decide if something is ready for a trip to the dry cleaners:

1. DOES IT HAVE AN UNPLEASANT ODOR? (SMELL THE ARMPITS. SERIOUSLY, PUT YOUR NOSE UP AGAINST THE FABRIC AND TAKE A WHIFF. IF SOMETHING OTHER THAN A SMILE CROSSES YOUR FACE, TAKE IT TO THE DRY CLEANERS.)

2. CHECK FOR STAINS. YOU ATE THAT DINNER THREE NIGHTS AGO, BUT ARE THE LEFTOVERS ON YOUR PANTS?

3. CHECK FOR WEAR AND TEAR, SUCH AS MISSING BUTTONS AND RIPPED SEAMS, ET CETERA.

If you've answered yes to any one of these three questions, dry cleaner, baby. Dry cleaner.

SWEATERS

- Use a special wool shampoo (regular detergents are too harsh) and either wash by hand in lukewarm water or put them in a mesh lingerie bag and use the gentle cycle of your washing machine.

- Don't wring out your sweaters—that's going to pull them out of shape. Instead, roll them in a towel to absorb excess water and then lay them flat to dry in a well-ventilated room.

- Gently reshape them (this is called blocking, by the way) so that they dry evenly. Note: You can wash all sweaters this way, including cashmere ones. In fact, you should avoid dry-cleaning cashmere—the chemicals can make it brittle.

LINGERIE AND BATHING SUITS

- Bras should be washed by hand in lukewarm water using delicate fabric wash.

- Slips, camisoles, and panties need delicate fabric wash, too, but they can go in the gentle cycle in the machine—just remember to use a mesh lingerie bag.

- Bathing suits should be washed by hand in cool water using delicate fabric wash after each wearing. If they've been exposed to chlorinated water, rinse them out as soon as possible.

SILK BLOUSES

- Wash by hand in lukewarm water using delicate fabric wash.

- Squeeze gently to remove excess water, then lay flat to dry.

JEANS

- Turn inside out and machine-wash in cold water.

- You can get special denim and darks detergents, both of which will help keep your denim dark and crisp.

- If they're old and fragile, wash by hand.

- Add one cup of white vinegar to your washing machine while the water is filling up, add detergent, and then add your jeans. The vinegar will protect the dye of your jeans.

WHITES

- Even professionally laundered shirts turn a little yellow or dingy after a while. Soak all your white shirts, pants, and skirts that are washable in hot water with a huge scoop of Oxi-Clean overnight. Set your washer to "wash" and leave the lid open. This allows it to agitate once (you can even agitate on delicate) and then sit in the water/Oxi-Clean overnight or at least two to four hours, then reset to agitate and close the lid for a full wash cycle. It will make your whites look whiter than ever. #WhiteHot

THE FOLLOWING ITEMS SHOULD BE DRY-CLEANED:

SUITS AND CLOTH COATS

- Dry-clean as infrequently as possible.

- Coats don't really need to be cleaned more than once a season depending on stains; suits will depend on how often they're worn.

- To keep garments fresh between cleanings, air out after each wearing, use a clothes brush, and spot clean as needed.

LEATHER AND SUEDE GARMENTS

■ Again, dry-clean as infrequently as possible.

■ In between dry cleanings, leather can be wiped with a damp cloth and a tiny amount of mild, nondetergent soap.

■ Suede brushes are excellent at keeping suede's nap looking fresh.

■ Light marks can be removed from suede with a new rubber pencil eraser.

BEADED AND EMBROIDERED PIECES

■ Take these on a case-by-case basis. When in doubt, check with your dry cleaner.

CLEANING EQUIPMENT

You probably have a washer, a dryer, and an iron so you think you're well equipped to take care of your clothes. And you are—to a point; however, there are a few extra pieces of equipment that can make the difference between looking good and looking great. Plus, all of these are easy to find online or in your local drugstore. And the best part? They're super affordable.

A GARMENT STEAMER: You know how your mother told you to hang a dress in the bathroom and run the shower to get the wrinkles out? Steamers work on the same principle, just much more efficiently, and you're not wasting water. Gentler than an iron and way faster, a steamer will get the wrinkles out of your clothes in seconds flat, which is why you'll find them on every fashion shoot. An inexpensive handheld steamer will also do the trick. (I'm talking under $20 for a portable handheld steamer—I've had two for 10 years; I keep one in my luggage and one at home.)

A NATURAL BRISTLE CLOTHES BRUSH: Clothes brushes remove dust and keep the fabric nap from looking matted down and tired. Never scrub with a clothes brush. Instead, sweep it lightly over a garment and always work in the same direction. To refresh clothes, brush them with a slightly damp—i.e., just-dipped-in-water—brush.

DE-FUZZING TAPE: I'm calling this de-fuzzing tape but you can use any wide, sticky tape to pick lint and hair off clothes. Just wrap it around your hand a few times and go to town. I personally use a lint roller, and I always keep one in the car.

SWEATER SHAVER: These little handy gadgets are affordable and work miracles on your sweaters. They remove fuzz and pilling, restoring your items to a like-new appearance.

TOUPEE TAPE: Do not bother with the double-sided tape they sell in lingerie stores—if you want your garment to stay in place, you need toupee tape. You can find it at any wig or costume store or, of course, at www.amazon.com. Nothing moves when you use this stuff.

EYELASH GLUE: For those times when toupee tape is too heavy-duty—I'm thinking of spaghetti straps that won't stay up—eyelash glue is indispensable.

IN THE BAG: WHAT'S IN LIZ'S STYLIST KIT?

WHEN THE PRESSURE IS ON, I'M LIKE A SURGEON WITH MY STYLIST KIT: I'VE GOT
SOMETHING FOR EVERY POSSIBLE EMERGENCY IN THERE, INCLUDING

A TIDE TO GO INSTANT STAIN REMOVER PEN FOR GETTING
WINE OFF OF WHITES, OR ANY SMALL STAIN MISHAPS.

SAFETY PINS FOR LAST-MINUTE MISHAPS AND ALL-OVER
DAMAGE CONTROL.

MAKEUP SPONGE FOR DEODORANT STAINS—ALWAYS CHECK
FOR THESE BEFORE LEAVING THE HOUSE, ESPECIALLY
WHEN YOU'RE WEARING BLACK. GENTLY SWIPE IT OVER
THE STAINED AREA, AND THE WHITE STREAKS WILL DISAPPEAR.

NAIL FILE FOR ANY LAST-MINUTE NAIL BREAKS OR ROUGH
SPOTS ON THE TIP OF YOUR FINGER. ROUGH SPOTS HAVE
A DOMINO EFFECT ON YOUR ENTIRE OUTFIT, SO DEAL WITH
THEM AS SOON AS THEY CROP UP.

A BLACK SHARPIE TO FIX SCUFFED BLACK SHOES.

DOWNY WRINKLE RELEASER TO SMOOTH OUT
STUBBORN WRINKLES.

CLEAR NAIL POLISH TO PREVENT FABRIC FROM FRAYING
OR TO STOP A RUN IN A PAIR OF HOSE OR TIGHTS.

COMMANDO LOW BEAMS NIPPLE COVERAGES
(WWW.BARENECESSITIES.COM) TO KEEP THE GIRLS
ON LOCKDOWN.

THAT'S JUST A PORTION OF THE THINGS I CARRY WITH ME WHEN I DO MY MAKEOVERS
AND AM ON SET. BUT DUE TO THE FACT THAT I'M NOT THERE WITH YOU EVERY MINUTE TO
SAVE THE DAY, I FOUND AN AMAZING TAKE-EVERYWHERE, FIT-IN-YOUR-PURSE EMERGENCY KIT
CALLED THE PINCH PROVISIONS (WWW.PINCHPROVISIONS.COM) THAT HAS 17 MUST-HAVES
FOR LAST-MINUTE WARDROBE MALFUNCTIONS. (FYI, I LOVE THESE PEOPLE; THEY'RE SO NICE.)

TOP FIVE TAKEAWAYS FROM LZ'S SECOND COMMANDMENT

ONE   IF YOU HAVE ITEMS IN YOUR CLOSET THAT YOU HAVEN'T WORN IN THREE YEARS OR PIECES THAT JUST DON'T FIT, DONATE THEM OR GIVE THEM AWAY.

TWO   WIRE HANGERS SHOULD BE AVOIDED AT ALL COSTS.

THREE   BUILD A WARDROBE OF CLASSIC PIECES BEFORE YOU START ADDING IN EXTRAS. NOTE: SHOP WITHIN YOUR BUDGET.

FOUR   STORE YOUR CLOTHES PROPERLY TO EXTEND THEIR LIFE SPAN.

FIVE   INSTEAD OF DRY CLEANING, SEE IF YOUR GARMENTS CAN BE HAND-WASHED TO SAVE TIME AND MONEY.

3

THOU SHALT
BE HEALTHY
INSIDE
AND OUT

"BEAUTY IS ONLY SKIN DEEP. I THINK WHAT'S
REALLY IMPORTANT IS FINDING A BALANCE OF
MIND, BODY, AND SPIRIT."

—JENNIFER LOPEZ

This book is all about how to create the perfect wardrobe, but if you really want to project the best version of yourself to the world, you have to be healthy, inside and out, hence the name of my third Perfect Wardrobe Commandment.

You know that saying, "It takes a village to raise a child"? Well, it definitely takes a village to make a celebrity look good, too! And I'm not talking about hair, makeup, and clothing—I'm talking about what it takes to create those perfect bodies that step into those top designer duds. They do *not* just wake up with those hot bods! From personal trainers to nutritionists, meditation coaches to yoga instructors, the kind of perfection you see on the red carpet requires a major, coordinated effort. And when I say major, I mean major.

"EVEN I DON'T WAKE UP LOOKING LIKE CINDY CRAWFORD"
— CINDY CRAWFORD

Over the years, I've had the opportunity to work with some of the best experts there are—i.e., the people who make up the "villages" that help each star look fit and fab—and I've learned a huge amount from them. In this chapter, it's now time for you to reap the benefits of their elite expertise.

After 15 years of doing makeovers, I've learned that what you see on the outside is a strong indication of what's happening on the inside. In this case, you actually can judge a book by its cover. Like we talked about in my First Commandment, in order to look good in your clothes, you have to feel good about yourself and truly love who you are. A huge part of feeling confident in your skin is making consistently healthy choices with your diet, getting regular exercise, and reducing stress through meditation.

The lovely Andie MacDowell, who looks just as good now as she did when she first hit the Hollywood scene, knows the importance of this. She drinks her water, wears her sunscreen, and works out regularly. "I give a lot of credit to my exercise regime for keeping me feeling and looking young," she told me. "I love to work out. Any kind of exercise I enjoy. I think it helps with my circulation and in keeping my skin looking healthy." #glowing

MY OWN PATH TO BETTER HEALTH

In the first chapter, I asked you to get naked, look in the mirror, and appreciate yourself for who you are. How can I honestly ask you to do something if I'm not willing to do it myself? Well, now it's my turn to stand in front of you and reveal my own path to better health.

As I told you earlier, I have a twin brother named Gregory who is seven minutes younger than I am. It always amazes us how fascinated people are by twins. Yes, it's wonderful and unique, but on the flip side, it can be extremely tough being compared to someone from day one. The frustrating part is that people tend to choose which twin they like better, whether in terms of who is better looking, who's nicer, who's sweeter, who's taller, who's thinner, who's in better shape . . . all of it.

For most of my life, I've struggled with weight issues and for a long time, I was the heavier twin. I think I subconsciously wanted to carve out my individual identity, and being heavier was my way of doing that—people knew when they looked at us that I was Lawrence, because I was heavier. Growing up, Gregory and I went to the same school, and when it came time to pick teams in PE, Gregory was always chosen first. I couldn't understand it. There we were—*identical*—so, what did he have that I didn't? Unfortunately, that feeling of being in second place plagued me for a long time.

Mind you, Gregory never did anything wrong or purposely tried to be better than me. On the contrary, he was also on his own journey to find out who he was. Feeling second was *my* issue, and I had to deal with it. I've come to realize the *best* part of having a twin is that I'm never alone and I will always have someone there who knows everything about me, supports me, loves me, and would do anything for me and I for him. *My* job was to find a way to stop comparing myself to him and create my own path and career. Had it not been for the "second place" feelings I had, and feeling "less than" my twin, I would never have embarked on this other journey to becoming The Fashion Guy.

Like anyone starting a new career knows, these things take time. After a tough year of putting myself out there, working hard and knocking on every door, I was finally given a shot on a local TV show here in LA, where I would host my own fashion segment. It was a hit, and my producers were thrilled. The wheels were in motion. I was on my way, and I couldn't have been happier. For the first time, this had nothing to do with being a twin; this was about me and *my* future. That little local TV show was my first stop, and before I knew it, I was making appearances on national shows and producers were actually calling me instead of the other way around. I was becoming my own person.

Then, everything came to a screeching halt. My mother was diagnosed with esophageal cancer, and died at the young age of 58. I was in my early thirties. This was a life-changing moment that altered the course of my life and career.

The facts are the facts and my mother had died because of poor health—she didn't exercise, she smoked two to three packs of cigarettes a day, she had an unhealthy diet, and, unfortunately, she struggled with alcoholism.

As I've gotten older and reflected on my mom's past, I totally understand why she had to use alcohol to numb herself from her pain. She was born during World War II in Berlin, and witnessed the horrors of war firsthand as a child. She eventually found her way to America in her late teens through a pre-arranged marriage that ended in physical abuse. While creating a new life on her own in Glendale, California, she was invited to a birthday party and that's where her life changed once again because she met my father at that party. And the rest, as they say, is *my* history.

When my mother died at such a young age, I was jolted into the reality of the preciousness of life and I decided it was time to make my life better and do everything she *hadn't*—exercise, eat right, and make my health a priority. The truth is: my mom had a disease; she was an alcoholic, and she didn't know how to find help. I understand that and I don't blame her for anything. My mom was amazing. She did the absolute best she could with what she knew and the tools she was given. She built her entire life around the three of us—her boys, Vincent, me, and Gregory. At 5'4" and a perfect size 4, she might have been small in stature, but her heart was huge and overflowing with enough love for all of us and our friends. I miss her like crazy and I'd give anything to hold her hand just one more time.

I lost a part of myself when I lost my mom. She was my go-to: my mother, my friend, my everything! And then—just like that—she was gone. I was broken, I was empty, and I was alone. I didn't know how to cope with it so I started making the wrong choices and found myself on a similar path as that of my mother's.

For over the five years following her death, I was on autopilot. I was blessed to be working consistently, but inside, I was emotionally empty and filling that void with all the wrong things. I was out of shape, eating the wrong foods, and indulging my addictions. My inner light was out. I was on the road to destruction and tempting fate by abusing my body. It wasn't until I hit rock bottom (twice) that I realized I had two choices: life or death.

I chose life.

I made a decision to acknowledge that I was powerless over certain things and that unless I stopped and turned my life over to God, I wasn't going to make it. I can proudly say that, by the grace of God, I am sober and following a 12-step program. And my life has never been better. I am truly blessed.

For four great years, my life was flowing beautifully—I was surrounded by supportive friends and family, and I was loving my work. I had found a new freedom and a new way to live. Life was good, but with the good often comes the bad; this time, however, I was better prepared for the bad news that was about to come crashing in . . .

On the exact same day, my father, Larry, and one of my best friends, Patty Fox, were both diagnosed with cancer. It was a day I'll never forget.

As for my relationship with my father, it had always been precarious. He was a very strong, powerful, dominant, and driven man, which makes sense when you consider the context of his rough childhood spent in a third world country. His father was an alcoholic and died when my dad was very young, making him the man of the house. In essence, he had to go from being a little boy to a man overnight.

As a teenager, he decided it was time for a new beginning, so he came to America. With only $20 in his pocket, my dad landed in Glendale, California— young, ambitious, and ready for a new life. With his strong sense of responsibility, as soon as he was financially able, he sent for his mother and sister (my Auntie Rima), so they could start their new lives in America as a family.

Little did he know that just a few years down the road, he would meet my mom on his birthday, fall in love, get married, and start building his own family. If his difficult past taught him anything, it was that he wanted to provide the foundation for his family that his father did not, and that meant doing whatever it took to be accountable and responsible. His intense, inner drive was a double-edged sword. Yes, it led to him owning his first piece of property at 18 years old, to becoming a successful business owner and real estate developer, and ultimately retiring in his early forties to become the first Armenian-American mayor of Glendale. He was a council member for 16 years and a celebrated mayor for four terms. He was a charismatic, gregarious man, revered by his peers and adored by the community. As a father, it was his intense energy and strength that put up a wall between us and prevented me from wanting to get close to him.

It pains me to say this, but for years, the last person I wanted to be around was my dad. It was his dominance and aggressive nature that pushed me away and closer to my mom, which was upsetting to my dad, who couldn't understand why I didn't want to be close to him.

But after my mother died and before my dad got sick, my relationship with him started to shift and the lines of communication opened. We had come to realize that we'd spent too many years not understanding each other, and it was time to give it a shot.

My father and I had breakfast every single Saturday because I was finally seeing my father through clear eyes and he was, in many ways, meeting his son for the first time. During those weekly meals, we talked about everything. I asked him questions about why he did what he did, what his parents taught him, what it was like being a parent, a husband, and my friend. I'm not going to lie; some of those conversations were tough and challenging, but it was through those difficult conversations that we were able to listen, learn, love, and move on from the past. During those moments that we shared, I learned that my father did the best he could with the hand he was dealt and that I was, indeed, a good son.

I truly believe that we all have an expiration date, and we don't know when God will take us. When my dad was diagnosed with cancer, this process of connecting was suddenly on the fast track. I believe when someone you love is diagnosed with a terminal disease like cancer, it sort of wakes you up and makes you see that your expiration date could be coming sooner than you expected.

While I was healing my relationship with my father, my relationship with my dear friend Patty deepened. Patty had been the fashion director of the Academy Awards® and the fashion doyenne of Los Angeles, a true fashionista, who had become one of my mentors. Everyone respected and adored Patty, and from day one, she believed in me and my potential. She was a bright light in my life, and when she looked at me, she only saw my greatness. We should all surround ourselves with people like that, who truly celebrate who we are.

Not only did Patty teach me a lot about "star style," she also taught me that true friendship feels *easy*—you don't have to work hard to maintain those deep friendships in life—and that sometimes the best moments are the quiet moments shared together. To me, Patty was invincible. I thought she would be here forever, but cancer had another plan. I watched this amazing, statuesque, beautiful woman wither away. She went home to God holding my hand and that of her best female friend, Paddy Calistro. The last words she uttered were "I love you." My life changed again in that moment. I could see clearly that time was running out, that I'd spent too long trying to be too many things to too many people and not being authentic with myself.

Patty was gone, but my father was still here and I realized that what had transpired in the past with him was just that—the past. I had to focus on celebrating the precious few moments we had left together. The aggressive form of blood cancer was taking him from us. In the final year of his life, we relished every minute together and just had fun. When my father died, he was surrounded by his family—I was at peace, he was at peace, we were at peace.

My father lived his life for his children. Everything he did was for us. Through those breakfasts, I came to understand that he was a product of his childhood and underneath all of it was an amazing man. Yes, I miss my dad but I miss the man who became my friend the most. He was my buddy, my champion. And I would give anything to have just one more of those breakfasts.

For those of you who are blessed to still have living parents, I really encourage you to find the time to sit with them and ask them questions, find out who they are and what they're all about. It can be tough, it can be tedious, and it can be painful. Trust me, I did it with both my parents, and both parents passed away with my hand in theirs. Those moments were peaceful, powerful, and perfect.

STARTING HERE, STARTING NOW

As I was coming to grips with my own mortality and understanding the importance of living a clean and healthy life, it was time for the outside to match the inside. While I was taking the necessary steps to build a solid inner, spiritual foundation, it was also time to focus on the physical and finally get in shape the right way. Timing is everything, and it was at this precise moment that I met celebrity trainer Craig Ramsay while I was hosting a show on the TV Guide Channel called *The Fashion Team*. In an instant, I knew he had something I wanted. From Craig's appearance, I could tell this man was in great shape; but it was the words he spoke and how he spoke them that resonated with me. Craig definitely showed up at the right time for me, and I call those moments "God shots."

I've been training with him now for over three years; I've lost 25 pounds and have done my best to keep it off. Do I have good days? Yes. Do I have bad days when I shovel food into my mouth and just can't stop emotionally eating? Yes. But what Craig has taught me is to not beat myself up and that I can always start again and make a healthier decision next time. It's not perfection I'm striving for; it's progress. Getting fit and eating right is a lifestyle, and everyone has a choice to be healthy. If you're reading this and wondering how you can do this, just stick with me and you'll meet some of the most talented experts in town who will give you the encouragement you need and the knowledge to get started.

Am I perfect? No way. But as much as I kick and scream through our workouts, I *feel* better. The world is a better place to me because I'm happy with myself and I see the world differently now. When you change, everything changes. This is partly because when it comes to exercise, I discovered that not only was I pushing my body and getting healthy, I was also having my own personal therapy session.

Exercise releases endorphins, and it gets your blood pumping and your mind racing. It lets you tap into your body   physically, mentally, emotionally, and spiritually—so those emotional reactions are common and needed. As a matter of fact, the other day I was at a spinning class, and I couldn't stop thinking about my parents. They've been gone for a while now, but something just happened and I couldn't stop crying. I miss my dad. I miss my mom. My only regret about this book is that they're not here celebrating with me. Now, I know that they're "above," watching and celebrating, but in that moment I just wanted them here with me physically. I'm glad that my twin, Gregory, was there with me in the class; he could relate and totally understand.

My body needed to experience the sadness and release it with my tears. It was truly a wonderful moment. And in that moment, I knew my parents were with me, loving me and celebrating me.

I truly believe that "getting healthy" is physical, mental, and spiritual. Our bodies hold on to emotions, and working out taps into those feelings and allows us to feel, process, and move on. It was definitely a perfect moment. I love you, Mom and Dad!

THE EXPERTS WEIGH IN

As I mentioned earlier in this chapter, I've been blessed to meet amazing people who are the best at what they do. I'm talking about the trainers and coaches to Hollywood royalty—from Oscar® and Emmy® winners to profes-

> "IT'S NEVER TOO LATE—NEVER TOO LATE TO START OVER, NEVER TOO LATE TO BE HAPPY."
> —JANE FONDA

sional athletes, Grammy® winners to Broadway stars—and if these tips work for them, they can certainly work for you. In order to motivate you, each one of my celebrated experts is sharing some of their quick tips, in their own words, to help you continue on your wellness journey or jump-start your program. #motivate

Before I let you hear from them, though, I want to give you some thoughts from my own experiences. Promise yourself that you'll do something physical every day. This can be as simple as taking a walk around the block or through the mall. Or vow to take the stairs instead of the elevator. Dance while you're cleaning the house or playing with your kids. Move your body. Love it and it will love you back, I promise.

As you know, Craig Ramsay is my personal trainer, but if hiring a trainer isn't realistic for you, then I encourage you to find a workout partner. This can be a best friend, a spouse, or a neighbor. Go with them to a local gym and have one of the certified trainers show you how everything works. Ask them to teach you the basics on the machines, the proper ways to spot, and anything else they think you should know. Pay attention, make notes, and learn. Another alternative is to join a gym facility like Curves, where there is a more structured atmosphere and you can work out practically every muscle in your body and burn a ton of calories over your lunch break. Check it out at www.curves.com. Working out with someone is not only fun, but it makes you accountable and makes you work just a little harder.

I believe that being healthy is one of the best choices you can make. So, while I go out for a hike, say hello to my fabulous experts and read their wise words of healthy advice.

CRAIG RAMSAY'S GET-YOUR-BUTT-IN-SHAPE-NOW TIPS

CRAIG RAMSAY, CELEBRITY FITNESS EXPERT AND MOVEMENT MOTIVATOR
WEBSITE: WWW.CRAIGRAMSAYFITNESS.COM
FACEBOOK: WWW.FACEBOOK.COM/CRAIGRAMSAYFITNESS
TWITTER: @CRAIGRAMSAYFIT
"5 MINUTE WORKOUT ANYWHERE" SERIES: WWW.ULIVE.COM/CRAIG-RAMSAY

BE OPEN TO NEW EXPERIENCES. Find the fitness and nutrition programs that will fit into your lifestyle. This means trying new workout programs until you find one that works for you.

BE ACCOUNTABLE. Share your goals and your program details with friends and family. Invite them to join you on this journey. If you don't have a support system with loved ones, then social media websites such as Twitter and Facebook can be a great source of support.

SET GOALS. Think of yourself as an athlete, and set an athlete's goals. For example, "I want to do my first 5K run in three months." When you strive to be your most athletic self, it is extremely motivating, plus you WILL see results weekly, monthly, and yearly. And remember, well-rounded athletes have to put their health and well-being first. (Moms: I know your kids are your priority, but if you take good care of yourself, you can take better care of them. And even if it's not a 5K, then go five times around the block or do a five-minute workout.)

THINK OUTSIDE THE GYM. I believe everyone should have an at-home exercise option. That eliminates the I-can't-get-to-the-gym excuse. Your home is your gym; like I say . . . "home *sweat* home," baby! You can work out with a DVD, or with a book like my *Anatomy of Stretching*, or you can have a more personalized Skype option. My clients make Skype appointments with me, or you can make a Skype date to workout with a friend.

MAKE EXERCISE PART OF YOUR SCHEDULE. Just as you do with a business meeting or a family commitment, put exercise in your calendar. If this sounds selfish, that's okay! If making yourself and your well-being a priority is selfish, then so be it. You're worth it.

When you're moving, you're exercising. You don't actually have to be within the walls of a gym or performing a specific "exercise" to be using your body. Move all day long with energy and purpose. Walk around your neighborhood or take a brisk stroll during your lunch hour. Even when you choose your vacations, pick destinations that will help you stay active, like camping, hiking, or rowing. You would be surprised at how many calories can be burned from walking all day at an amusement park!

KEEP THE MOTIVATION GOING. To stay motivated, try calling your own phone and leaving yourself an encouraging message. Ask your loved ones to do the same and then listen to these messages during those trying, tiring times when you need a little extra support. Another way I like to stay motivated is to put an event on my calendar every few months that I want to look good for, like a swimsuit beach day, a pool party, a family photo, or a get-together with friends.

CELEBRATE YOURSELF. Take it one day at a time and be proud of what you're able to do physically each day.

ASHLEY BORDEN'S TIPS FOR GETTING FIT FOR LIFE

ASHLEY BORDEN, CELEBRITY FITNESS CONSULTANT AND TV PERSONALITY
WEBSITE: WWW.ASHLEYBORDEN.COM
YOUTUBE CHANNEL: WWW.YOUTUBE.COM/USER/ASHLEYBORDENFITNESS

PLAY DETECTIVE WITH YOURSELF. You need to know what's going on in your life to get a grip on it. Get a physical every year so your doctor can monitor what's happening internally. At home, keep track of your eating habits. Look in your cabinets and refrigerator and throw away anything that has partially hydrogenated oil in the ingredients, along with every can of soda.

PICK UP A BARBELL—FOR REAL. Ladies, if you are not incorporating at least two to three days of heavier strength training into your routine, you're not getting enough of a workout. Start out with a light weight such as two pounds, and as you get stronger, start using more challenging weight like five, eight, and ten pounders. Your body will guide you.

Burn calories efficiently. Women need to incorporate body-weight moves to get a complete workout. Build functional strength and reduce body fat with these exercises:

- SQUATS
- LUNGES (side, reverse, walking)
- PULL-UPS (overhand grip and underhand grip)—Begin with machine assistance or bands, then graduate to full body weight and eventually hanging weight with your own body weight.
- PUSH-UPS (on knees or full body)—Once a full body push-up is mastered, you can use a stability ball, single leg, and offset hand placement to vary your push-up challenge.

CREATE SUPPORT. Ideally, we'd all have the support of our friends, roommates, neighbors, et cetera. If it's not there, you need to make it happen by reaching out and asking for it. A friend, relative, or even your doggie can make following through with training dates, dog walks, or even healthy grocery-store shopping easier. Better choices are easier to make with the support of someone who wants you to succeed.

HEALTHY EATING IS NOT A DIET; IT'S A LIFESTYLE CHOICE. Healthy eating is not about following a diet for a few months and then giving it up. Create the habit of good food choices and make them a part of your life. I created my S.O.S. Food Plan (you can read about it in my book, *Your Perfect Fit*) as well as the option of my clean, organic vegan, vegetarian, or flexitarian food delivery service to help people find a healthy balance of consciousness and control with their food.

BREAK OUT OF YOUR COMFORT ZONE. I mean that both mentally and physically. I started Brazilian jujitsu and Olympic lifting in my forties! Learning a new sport has given me a great sense of pride, accomplishment, and capability. The physical effect it had on my physique was just an incredible bonus. You could try enrolling in intramural sports in your area or check sites like Groupon (www.groupon.com) for great starter deals in all things athletic! Or try my LivestrongWoman "Perfect Form" In-Home Training series—all the workouts are under 20 minutes long.

NICK HOUNSLOW'S TIPS TO SPIN YOURSELF THIN

NICK HOUNSLOW, CELEBRITY TRAINER AND SPIN INSTRUCTOR
TWITTER & INSTAGRAM: @NICKHOUNSLOW

DEFINITION OF SPINNING: Biking on a stationary bike, typically in a group setting, with blood-pumping music at the gym or a spin studio, where you control the resistance on the bike.

YOU NEED TO HEART YOUR HEART. Spinning is a great cardiovascular and resistance workout that's very low impact and great for all ages and sizes.

GET YOUR GROUP ON. Exercising as part of a group is a wonderful way to get through the pain. Knowing that they're struggling as much as you are and that you are not alone is really helpful. There is such an amazing sense of camaraderie in my room. Everyone is cheering for the new people.

IT'S A MIND GAME. The meditation at the beginning of class and the cooldown phase at the end are great ways to relax. They give your mind and body a chance to calm down in order to relieve built-up stress. Indoor cycling builds mental strength. When you're on a bike, there are good and bad days. The key is to push through the bad ones. The mental self-discipline gained in cycling can be used in all aspects of your life. Personally, it gives me a stronger sense of self and it's an instant shot of self-esteem. It makes me feel like I can conquer the world.

BE REAL. HAVE REALISTIC GOALS! So many people go full force and change everything at once. Then, after a month, they crash and end up back at square one. If you start small, the task at hand will never seem that daunting. So as you tackle each milestone, you will feel proud and remain positive. It will be that much easier to leap to the next challenge!

10 COMMANDMENTS 93

ROSS RAYBURN'S TIPS ON GETTING DOWN WITH A DOWNWARD DOG

ROSS RAYBURN, INTERNATIONAL YOGA INSTRUCTOR
WEBSITE: WWW.ROSSRAYBURN.COM
TWITTER: @ROSSRAYBURN

IT'S A WHOLE BODY/MIND THING. I still semi-jokingly give credit to Madonna and Sting for making yoga so mainstream back in the nineties. But my guess is that yoga's popularity is a part of the evolution of fitness coinciding with a global awareness of other cultures, like the beliefs of Eastern philosophy. From a philosophical perspective, I see our culture moving toward a greater sense that physical health and mental health are interwoven. Yoga is a perfect way to access both simultaneously.

STRETCHING THE POINT. For me, there's no difference between yoga and stretching. However, pure stretching is geared toward a purely physical pursuit, whereas yoga in general is geared toward the physical, mental, and oftentimes spiritual aspects of who we are. The secret to becoming more flexible is not stretching; it's getting strong in places where you're weak.

IT'S THE THINKING PERSON'S EXERCISE. First, I should state the obvious and say I'm biased and that yoga is a great form of exercise. In fairness, I readily recognize that a typical yoga class is not for everyone. That said, I fell in love with yoga precisely because I love to exercise and I'm insatiably curious. So when I found a form of exercise where I was asked to think and sweat at the same time, I was hooked.

JUST DO IT. The best way to find a good teacher is to ask friends and coworkers for recommendations, and then just start taking classes. Go to as many different types of yoga classes and try out as many different teachers as you can. When a class feels good and a teacher resonates with you, you'll know. Just make sure your yoga teacher is aware of how to avoid injuries.

EMILY FLETCHER'S TIPS ON EXERCISING YOUR MIND FOR THE GOOD OF YOUR BODY

EMILY FLETCHER, MEDITATION TEACHER AND EXPERT

FACEBOOK: WWW.FACEBOOK.COM/ZIVAMEDITATION

TWITTER: @ZIVAMEDITATION

INSTAGRAM: @EMILYZIVA

ONLINE MEDITATION TRAINING: WWW.ZIVAMIND.COM

LIVE MEDITATION TRAINING IN NYC & LA: WWW.ZIVAMEDITATION.COM

MEDITATION IS NOT JUST FOR PATCHOULI-WEARING HIPPIES. Meditation is a powerful, stress-relieving tool. We, as a society, have managed to get out of balance. When we aren't working, we're obsessively watching others live their lives through social media. This leaves very little time for real connection or the "right now." And guess where your bliss and fulfillment hang out. In the "right now"! Every spiritual text has been saying this since the beginning of time. What you seek is in you. Well, that's fine to understand as a concept, but it is much more powerful to actually experience it every day. This is what meditation gives us: an all-access pass to our own fulfillment in the only place that it actually resides . . . in the right now.

DON'T JUST ASSUME YOU KNOW HOW TO DO IT. The reason most people have a hard time getting started with meditation is because we assume we know how. People think meditation is just sitting in a chair, closing your eyes, and giving your mind a command to stop thinking. That's impossible. No one can give their mind a command to stop thinking! We have to reframe our perception of meditation. Meditation is like any other skill. It takes a bit of practice and a good teacher. This doesn't mean you have to find a guru; any teacher worth their salt will give you tools that will make you self-sufficient.

IT'S ALL ABOUT STYLE. Many popular styles of meditation were designed for monks, not for people with busy minds and lives. The technique I teach was made for people like us—people who have jobs and live in society. It's referred to as Nishkam Karma Yoga (union attained by least effort), or as I lovingly call it, "the lazy man's meditation." In this style of meditation, you are given a mantra and this mantra does the heavy lifting for you. It de-excites the nervous system and gives the body very deep rest (deeper than sleep!). You come out on the other side feeling like you had a mini vacation or a supercharged power nap.

MAKE A COMMITMENT. In the beginning, you have to make meditating non-negotiable and schedule it like you would any other task, but after a while you won't be able to imagine your life without it. I love the way I feel after I meditate. I feel more like myself: grounded, clear, brighter. And I get a lot more done. If you know what you're doing, meditation isn't a chore; it's a pleasure. It is easy to commit to a piece of dark chocolate every day, because you want it, you look forward to it. Meditation is like that for me, and if you give it a shot, it can help you say good-bye to stress and all of its ugly side effects. I no longer see life as a race I need to win. Instead, I see it as a lovely playground for me to use my gifts to help lift others up. When you have access to energy from an inexhaustible source, helping people becomes a joy, not a chore.

TOP FIVE TAKEAWAYS FROM LZ'S THIRD COMMANDMENT

ONE   MOVE YOUR BODY EVERY DAY, EVEN IF IT'S JUST TAKING THE STAIRS INSTEAD OF THE ELEVATOR OR WALKING A FEW BLOCKS.

TWO   FIND A WORKOUT PARTNER TO MAKE WORKING OUT FUN AND TO KEEP YOU ACCOUNTABLE. (YOU CAN ALSO DO THIS OVER SKYPE.)

THREE   SURROUND YOURSELF WITH PEOPLE WHO LOVE AND CELEBRATE YOU FOR WHO YOU ARE.

FOUR   GET YOUR FIT ON AND TRY SOMETHING NEW, WHETHER IT'S WEIGHT TRAINING, A SPIN CLASS, OR YOGA.

FIVE   IF YOU ARE STRUGGLING WITH ANY TYPE OF ADDICTION, THE FIRST STEP IS TO ADMIT IT TO YOURSELF, THEN REACH OUT FOR HELP, AND THE REST WILL FALL INTO PLACE. #GOD

4 | THOU SHALT DRESS FOR STYLE, NOT SIZE

"DON'T BE INTO TRENDS. DON'T MAKE FASHION OWN YOU,
BUT YOU DECIDE WHAT YOU ARE, WHAT YOU WANT TO EXPRESS
BY THE WAY YOU DRESS AND THE WAY YOU LIVE."

—GIANNI VERSACE

■ For a lot of women, fashion really boils down to a numbers game. Come on, you know what I mean. Every time you go shopping, there is a set of figures floating around in your head that are so complicated even Albert Einstein would have trouble keeping them straight! You're thinking about your current weight, how much you used to weigh, your ideal weight, your waist measurement, your dress size, the dress size you fantasize about being . . . I mean, seriously, I could go on forever because I totally get it.

Listen, I'm no mathematician and we're not here to chat about trigonometry, so let's give the mental numbers a rest! It's not the number that's going to make you look good; it's the fit. Did you just have an "aha" moment? Good! Now, throw those numbers out the window and understand that no matter your size, what really matters is how your clothes fit you.

This is a tough concept for a lot of women to grasp, and no wonder! There is a persistent, widespread belief that if you're a size 12, you will automatically look better if you're a smaller size, like 10 or lower. The bottom line is that women get psychologically attached to what is essentially a meaningless digit. You know what I'm talking about. Have you ever forced yourself into a pair of jeans that clearly didn't fit just so you could have that certain size on the label? Remove those labels! And never, ever tell anyone what size your pants are; really, it's none of their business. I can see you at this moment nodding your head in agreement, and laughing at yourself about it—this is so you, right? I've seen it more times than I care to remember, and I am here to tell you that thinking that way is crazy! Would you rather wear a dress with a certain number on it instead of one that makes you look amazing, regardless of size? I think not!

"I KNOW WHAT WOMEN WANT. THEY WANT TO BE BEAUTIFUL."
—VALENTINO

There is no point in being married to a size—for one thing, it's going to change from designer to designer and cut to cut. For another thing, who cares? No one, I repeat, no one is going to ask you to take off your dress and show them the label, and if they do, you should smack them.

THE RIGHT FIT AND HOW TO GET IT

Instead of blindly shopping for (and obsessing about) a size, start shopping for a flattering fit. If you've been in the habit of just grabbing sizes rather than styles and beelining for the dressing room, this will take some mental adjustment. Yves Saint Laurent, a god among designers, knew what he was talking about when he said that dressing is a way of life. He understood that in order to get it right, you have to devote some time to it. But, I promise, it will be worth it when you see the results.

When you go shopping, stop thinking about the number/size and start thinking about the style because, again, IT'S ALL ABOUT THE FIT!

"EFFORTLESS ELEGANCE. BEING SEXY IS AN EXPRESSION OF YOUR STYLE AND PERSONALITY. A WOMAN WITH STYLE IS UNFORGETTABLE."
—CATHERINE MALANDRINO

CLOTHES THAT FIT SHOULD:

- Have shoulder seams that correspond to your actual shoulders.
- Neither pull nor gape across the bust.
- Have buttons that button and zippers that zip without insane efforts, such as hopping, sucking in, holding your breath, dancing around the bedroom, et cetera.
- Be the correct length for your arms and legs, neither too short nor too long.
- Be comfortable to sit, stand, walk, and stretch in.

WHEN A TAILOR NEEDS TO TINKER WITH YOUR CLOTHES

The reality is, for many of us, it's hard to create an entire wardrobe with the perfect fit. But there's no reason you can't take your clothing and have it tailor-made for you. Yes, it's true. A tailor truly doesn't cost a fortune and can take your wardrobe and make it look as if it was custom-made for you. Often you can find a more affordable tailor at your local cleaners. Many fabric stores also have seamstresses for hire who can save you money and make your fit perfect.

TAILOR-MADE: LZ'S LIST OF HOW TAILORS CAN WORK MAGIC

1   CREATE THE ILLUSION OF A NARROWER WAIST BY NIPPING IN JACKETS AND FITTING SKIRTS TO YOUR WAIST

2. HEM SKIRTS SO THEY ARE AGE-APPROPRIATE AND FIGURE-FLATTERING— EITHER AN INCH ABOVE OR AN INCH BELOW THE KNEE. IN YOUR TWENTIES, YOU CAN GO SHORTER TO A MINI STATUS.

3. HEM TROUSERS AND JEANS—DON'T THINK THAT JUST BECAUSE JEANS ARE WORN IN A MORE CASUAL WAY THAT THEY DON'T DESERVE TAILORING.

4. SHORTEN JACKETS THAT ARE TOO LONG FOR YOUR FORM.

5. GIVE "STRAIGHT" OR A-LINE SKIRTS A SEXY PENCIL SILHOUETTE WITHOUT BEING TOO TIGHT.

6. REPLACE WORN-OUT LININGS IN JACKETS AND COATS—A NICE LITTLE TRICK THAT GIVES OLD FAVORITES NEW LIFE.

7. ASK THE TAILOR IF IT'S WORTH ALTERING A CERTAIN ITEM—A GOOD TAILOR WILL TELL YOU THE TRUTH

If you've never taken anything to a tailor before, you're in for a life-changing experience. Seriously. Good tailors are nothing short of miracle workers. They can make you look taller, slimmer, and fitter. The best way to find the best tailor for you is to ask around. Check with your favorite salesperson or the best boutique in town and ask them who they use. Ask your well-dressed friends. Read online reviews (though, remember, it's easier to give a bad review than a good one). You might want to test a tailor out with something simple first, like shortening a skirt. If you like the experience and feel they did a good job, put your clothing in their hands. #TailorMade

> "FIT IS TO FASHION, AS LOCATION IS TO REAL ESTATE."
> —KAUFMANFRANCO

"FIGURING" IT OUT

When I set out to write this book, I wanted to keep it simple because really, there is no reason to make good style overly complicated. Basically, if you're a woman, you're probably going to fall into one of five categories. There are plenty of names for these various shapes, but here's how I like to think of them:

- **THE CLASSIC:** aka the hourglass, the pinup girl.
- **THE BOOTY BOUNTIFUL:** aka the pear, the triangle.
- **THE TOP OF THE LINE:** aka the apple, the inverted triangle.
- **THE STREAMLINED:** aka the boyish, the rectangle.
- **ENCEINTE AND APRÈS ENCEINTE:** For those of you who are expecting or have recently delivered a little bundle of joy, "enceinte" is French for pregnant and "après enceinte" means post-pregnant. (I had to throw in a little French because some things just sound better in French. Oui? Oui!)

Now, let's discuss the categories; in order to give you visuals, I've also thrown in some celebrity names as examples.

THE CLASSIC

SOFIA VERGARA, SALMA HAYEK, MARIAH CAREY

If you're a Classic, your bust and hips are approximately the same size and your waist is about nine inches smaller. Your bust is full and your legs are shapely—lucky you! But before you get too smug, remember this: Curves can veer from tasteful to trashy in the blink of an overly tight corset top. Be careful! Historically, the hourglass has been considered the "ideal" body type. Think: Marilyn Monroe, Sophia Loren, and all those deliciously curvy stars of the 1950s. Of course in the 1950s, clothes were cut for curves. Nowadays, that's not always the case, which can make dressing luscious proportions a challenge. The key to dressing an hourglass figure is to show off your small waist while keeping the rest of you in proportion.

First and foremost, do not try to camouflage what nature gave you with baggy, shapeless clothes. You'll just end up looking big all over. Instead, enhance those sexy curves with tailored—note I said tailored, not tight—dresses, blouses, and skirts. Pants and jeans are going to present your biggest challenges. They're not going to be impossible to find, but you're going to have to put in more effort.

THE CLASSIC SHOULD LOOK FOR:

- Pencil skirts
- Tailored jackets and coats that accentuate the waist
- Thick belts that show off your waist
- Thin, soft fabrics that drape

AVOID LIKE THE PLAGUE:

- Skinny jeans
- Baby-doll tops and dresses
- Low-cut trousers of any kind
- Blouson cuts and peasant blouses
- Ruffles, bows, and anything else that adds bulk to your beautiful breasts
- Anything that cuts off at the hip
- Stiff, bulky fabrics

THE BOOTY BOUNTIFUL

JENNIFER LOPEZ, EVA LONGORIA, KATE WINSLET

Booty Bountiful ladies have luscious hips and rears, narrow shoulders, and bustlines that are smaller in comparison to the curviness of their lower bodies. You're the ones who turn around in the fitting room and ask, "Does this make my butt look big?" (If you have to ask, then, yes, it does. You're welcome.)

Thanks to women who like to showcase their rear view, this figure has been getting a lot of play lately. To make the most of your enviably small waist and narrow, feminine shoulders, you need to call attention to your upper half while downplaying what's down below. Darker skirts and pants are more flattering, while white and light colors make you look fuller. This basic fashion rule will never fail to guide you.

Patterned blouses, bold-statement necklaces, and dramatic necklines should all be part of your dressing strategies. Unfriend below-the-waist prints, mini-skirts, and tapered pants. Save the drama for up top, and on your lower half go with dark, neutral, and subdued hues, anything that does not draw the eye to your butt.

THE BOOTY BOUNTIFUL SHOULD LOOK FOR:

- Light-colored tops and blouses
- Jackets that cover your hips (just remember to look for a nipped-in waist)
- Boatneck tops and dresses
- Wrap tops and dresses

AVOID LIKE THE PLAGUE:

- Loose, baggy clothes
- Bias-cut skirts and dresses
- Skinny jeans
- Pants with any kind of detailing (grommets, contrast stitching, pleats, cuffs, etc.)
- Skirts and pants made of shiny fabrics

THE TOP OF THE LINE

JESSICA SIMPSON, JENNIFER HUDSON, HELEN MIRREN

My Top of the Line lovelies, you have gorgeous va-va-voom breasts, a less defined waist, wide shoulders, and narrow hips. Your deck is stacked to be top-heavy, which can make it seem like the "girls" are on a mission to break free from their restraints and run out into the world. Don't let it happen!

Your dressing strategy is all about creating a longer, leaner torso, which will, in turn, make you look longer and leaner. The best way to do this is to hike the girls up and put them on display. You want to create as much space as possible between the bust and the hips, something that's hard to do if your breasts are hanging out around your midsection. I'm going to go into more detail about bras in a minute, but for you—a properly fitted bra is key. Sagginess means allover bagginess, and that's something we want to avoid, like acid-washed jeans at a black-tie event (or, come to think of it, acid-washed jeans anywhere).

THE TOP OF THE LINE SHOULD LOOK FOR:

- A really good support bra
- Fabrics that skim your curves rather than cling to them
- Bootcut jeans
- Jackets and tops that finish either above or below the waist area
- V-neck tops (the most flattering neckline for a large bust)
- Scoop-neck tops
- A-line skirts

AVOID LIKE THE PLAGUE:

- Empire-waist tops and dresses
- Long, dangling necklaces
- Skinny jeans
- Shoulder pads
- Embellishments on tops and jackets

THE STREAMLINED

SARAH JESSICA PARKER, GWEN STEFANI, KATE MOSS

Streamlined ladies may be petite or tall, but what unites them is their slim, lean shape. You're more angular than curvy, and at this particular moment in history that makes you the fashion lottery winner because most designer clothes are cut with you in mind, all fashion trends look good on you, and you have no problem finding flattering jeans.

However, this type of woman often wants to add a few curves to her contours. This is one of the easier tricks to pull off. Essentially, you want to create the illusion of volume where there is none: peplums, gathered bustlines, skirts that flare out over the hips—all of these are surefire curv-ifiers. (See? I made a fashion funny!) Use belts to define your waist. Soft shapes and ultra-feminine details like ruffles look great on you and never look overdone. There isn't much you can't wear. #LuckyYou

THE STREAMLINED SHOULD LOOK FOR:

- Ruffles and frills that soften an angular frame
- Horizontal stripes, which can create the illusion of curves
- Dresses in soft fabrics like chiffon
- Bootcut and flared jeans
- Belts that add definition to your waist

AVOID LIKE THE PLAGUE:

- Large prints that can overwhelm your small frame
- Itty-bitty jewelry
- Straight-up-and-down dresses
- Vertical stripes

ENCEINTE AND APRÈS ENCEINTE (PREGNANT AND POST-PREGNANT)

KATE MIDDLETON, NATALIE PORTMAN, BEYONCÉ

There's no other period in a woman's life quite like pregnancy. You're literally blooming. Your skin glows. You're giddy with excitement.

On the other hand, you may also have swollen feet and ankles and lower back pain, and you've just gained a lot of weight. But don't panic, mommies!

The most important thing is to take care of yourself, eat healthy, take care of that bundle of joy, and remember that wearing a muumuu for nine months is no way to walk the road of maternity.

You may think that shapeless, baggy clothes camouflage your expanding waistline, but that is simply not the case. Maternity wear of yesterday is gone; now, so many designers have jumped on the mommy-to-be bandwagon and have designed clothing with the baby bump in mind . . . you can be pregnant, put-together, and chic.

You don't need to wear skintight clothes, but make sure your outfits show the shape of your back and shoulders or you risk looking larger than life. Maternity jeans have come a long way since those ugly elastic panels back in the eighties, and I strongly urge all moms-to-be to get a pair or two, if that's an option for your budget. They work post-baby, too, when you're still getting your figure back!

ENCEINTE AND APRÈS ENCEINTE SHOULD LOOK FOR:

- Belts to cinch just above the belly—an easy way to give your figure some definition
- Stretch fabric tops and dresses with Lycra
- Tops that gather under the bust to accentuate the cleavage
- Well-cut maternity jeans (J Brand and A Pea in the Pod both cut a great pair.)

AVOID LIKE THE PLAGUE:

- Tent dresses
- Dresses that are too short
- Anything that doesn't fit across the back
- Stiff fabrics

IF YOU HAVEN'T BEEN A FAN OF LYCRA BEFORE, PREGNANCY

IS WHEN YOU WILL REALLY APPRECIATE ITS TRANSFORMATIVE

POWER. SERIOUSLY, IT'S A PREGNANCY WARDROBE SUPERHERO.

MY GOOD FRIEND, LISA KARAMARDIAN, MD, IS AN OBSTETRICIAN

AND GYNECOLOGIST WITH PACIFIC WOMEN'S HEALTH CARE

ASSOCIATES IN NEWPORT, CALIFORNIA, AND WHEN I ASKED HER

ABOUT SHAPEWEAR DURING PREGNANCY, SHE SAID THAT IT'S

PERFECTLY SAFE IN THE FIRST TRIMESTER BECAUSE THE BABY IS IN A

FLUID-FILLED ENVIRONMENT. SHE SAID IN THE SECOND TRIMESTER,

MATERNITY SHAPEWEAR WILL BE YOUR BEST FRIEND AND GIVE YOU

A SMOOTHER SILHOUETTE IN ALL YOUR CLOTHES, AND IT WILL

EASE THE PRESSURE ON YOUR LOWER BACK. NEAR THE END OF

YOUR PREGNANCY, SHE SAYS SHAPEWEAR CAN BE VERY HELPFUL

AT PROVIDING ADDITIONAL SUPPORT, PREVENTING SWELLING,

AND HELPING WITH CIRCULATION. SHE ALSO SAYS TO ALWAYS

PICK A FABRIC THAT BREATHES IN ORDER TO PREVENT YEAST INFEC-

TIONS. CHECK OUT WWW.SPANX.COM FOR THEIR FULL LINE OF

MATERNITY SHAPEWEAR OR WWW.DESTINATIONMATERNITY.COM.

THINK TWO HIGH-HEEL STEPS AHEAD

With this chapter focusing on style instead of size, beautiful style means making sure your outfit is picture perfect. This is your chance to discover wardrobe malfunctions before you leave the house, because these aren't fashion "goofs" you want to catch in the bathroom mirror at work. Have you missed a belt loop? Is your underwear showing? Do you have that dreaded panty line? Or is your "whale tail"

> "SIMPLICITY IS THE ULTIMATE SOPHISTICATION."
> —LEONARDO DA VINCI

(aka thong) sticking out of the top of your jeans? If you answered "yes" to any of these questions, now is your chance to remedy the situation by fixing it fast.

So, how do you take good style to great style in one quick decision? It really comes down to what I call the "third piece." This is the item that pulls your whole look together and makes it yummy. It could be an amazing statement necklace. It could be a brand-new leather bomber jacket. It could be a great bag or a multicolored scarf. Whatever it is, it shouldn't be competing for attention with everything else you're wearing. Give the third piece some air to breathe and some space to shine and it will make your entire outfit look oh-so-stunning.

SNAP A SELFIE!

One thing I do with all my makeovers is take photos of them in several outfits. If I look at the photo and my eye goes to the dress and not the face, I change the dress. I truly believe that one should never fight the face—it's your most beautiful asset. Your best compliment should be, "you look gorgeous," not "cool dress." It's not about what you're wearing as much as it is about your overall look. Are you the focus? I hope so, because you deserve to be.

This photo technique is also super useful when you aren't sure what bra to wear. It's so easy to do this at home. Turn on your camera's flash, set the timer for 15 seconds, pose, and voilà, instant results. Take a look at the photo and you can see what everyone else will be seeing when they look at you. This photo will also show you trouble spots to be fixed or adjusted. Is the bra visible through the shirt? Is it pooching out some back fat? #PhotosNeverLie

BUILDING YOUR FASHION FOUNDATION

You know what makes celebrities look good? Well, lots of things, but for my money, it all starts with shapewear. Every red-carpet look is built on shapewear. That's why every single makeover I do begins with these all-important wardrobe staples.

If you're not yet a convert to the miracle that is modern shapewear, it may be because you associate it with your grandmother's girdle. Honey, those days are so over! Today's shapewear is not the ironclad torture device of yesteryear. It's comfortable. Moreover, it comes in an assortment of styles and colors that will sculpt and slim every part of you. You can whittle your waist, lift your ladies, resculpt your rear, tighten your thighs, and carve away your calves, and nobody's the wiser.

FASHION FOUNDATION #1:
THE PROPER BRA

Let's face it; not all boobs are created equal. Sometimes, as the French say, il y a du monde au balcon. The direct translation is "the balcony is crowded," but the real meaning is "whoa, that's some rack!" Other times, the balcony is deserted. But no matter what God gave you, the right bra can make all the difference, and it truly has the power to make you and your outfit go from "blah" to "bam!"

"BREAST" IN CLASS

WHEN IT COMES TO BRAS, I THINK YOU NEED A MINIMUM OF THREE STYLES: A WORKOUT BRA, A T-SHIRT BRA, AND A CONVERTIBLE BRA (ONE THAT LETS YOU MOVE THE SHOULDER STRAPS TO ACCOMMODATE STRAPLESS, CRISSCROSS, HALTERS, AND ONE-SHOULDER TOPS OR DRESSES). IF YOU'RE EITHER WELL-ENDOWED OR ON THE SMALLER SIDE, YOU NEED SPECIAL ATTENTION.

HERE ARE MY RECOMMENDATIONS FOR ALL OF THE ABOVE AT LOW, MEDIUM, AND HIGH PRICE POINTS.

BRAS FOR BIGGER BUSTS:

LOW: VANITY FAIR BEAUTIFUL BENEFITS FULL FIGURE BRA, APPROXIMATELY $21, WWW.BARENECESSITIES.COM

MEDIUM: BALI DOUBLE SUPPORT BRA, APPROXIMATELY $36, WWW.JCPENNEY.COM

HIGH: WACOAL RETRO CHIC FULL FIGURE UNDERWIRE BRA, APPROXIMATELY $60, WWW.ESSENTIALAPPAREL.COM

BRAS FOR SMALLER BUSTS:

LOW: WACOAL PETITE BANDEAU UNDERWIRE BRA, APPROXIMATELY $31, WWW.ESSENTIALAPPAREL.COM

MEDIUM: WACOAL SEAMLESS SOFT CUP MESH BRA, APPROXIMATELY $42, WWW.NORDSTROM.COM

HIGH: LULA LU PETITES SABINE LACE BRA, APPROXIMATELY $56, WWW.LULALU.COM

WORKOUT BRAS:

LOW: C9 BY CHAMPION WOMEN'S SEAMLESS RACER BRA, APPROXIMATELY $17, WWW.TARGET.COM

MEDIUM: NIKE RUNNING PRO COMBAT WORKOUT BRA,
APPROXIMATELY $30, WWW.DILLARDS.COM

HIGH: MOVING COMFORT JUNO SPORTS BRA,
APPROXIMATELY $56, WWW.MOVINGCOMFORT.COM

T-SHIRT BRAS:

LOW: JOCKEY T-SHIRT BRA,
APPROXIMATELY $15, WWW..JOCKEY.COM

MEDIUM: DKNY FUSION T-SHIRT BRA,
APPROXIMATELY $42, WWW.BELK.COM

HIGH: LA PERLA INVISIBLE FEELING T-SHIRT BRA,
APPROXIMATELY $92, WWW.HERROOM.COM

CONVERTIBLE BRAS:

LOW: AMOUREUSE MOLDED CONVERTIBLE BRA,
APPROXIMATELY $30, WWW.FULLBEAUTY.COM

MEDIUM: JEZEBEL LACE ATTRACTION 7 WAY CONVERTIBLE BRA,
APPROXIMATELY $34, WWW.HERROOM.COM

HIGH: LE MYSTERE DOS NU CONVERTIBLE BRA,
APPROXIMATELY $56, WWW.BAGSHOP.COM

AND FOR THOSE SPECIAL OCCASIONS WHEN YOU WANT TO GET
YOUR SEXY ON, GO FOR A PADDED, PUSH-UP BRA AND TAKE THE
"GIRLS" OUT FOR A WALK. SOME OPTIONS I RECOMMEND ARE:

LOW: INSPIRATIONS WOMEN'S DOUBLE TAKE EXTREME PUSH UP BRA,
APPROXIMATELY $15, WWW.SEARS.COM

MEDIUM: THE WONDER BRA,
APPROXIMATELY $35, WWW.WONDERBRA.COM

HIGH: BOMBSHELL PUSH UP BRA,
APPROXIMATELY $60, WWW.VICTORIASSECRET.COM

THE RIGHT FIT

Okay, let's talk fit. Remember: just like in clothes, it's not the size, it's the fit that matters! Don't get all hung up on where you land in the alphabet—it just doesn't matter because no one's checking your cup size at the door.

When it comes to choosing the perfect bra, have a professional bra fitting. WARNING: Do not attempt this at home. Nor should you Google "how to find the perfect-fitting bra" and go from there. The Internet is good for many things; determining your bra size is not one of them. For this, you need to get up close and personal with a professional, and don't think this is a do-it-once-and-get-it-over-with deal. The average woman wears something like seven different bra sizes in her lifetime. Breast size changes with weight gain and loss, during and after pregnancy, and with age. To make sure you're always wearing the correct size, get an annual bra fitting; it's an hour out of your year. Many department stores have a fit specialist on staff. These services are fabulous and free. Are you really going to tell me you don't have time for that?

YOUR CUP RUNNETH OVER: THE "WILLS" AND "WON'TS" OF A GOOD BRA FITTER:

A BRA FIT SPECIALIST WILL:

- FIRST AND FOREMOST, MEASURE YOU WITH A MEASURING TAPE.
- WORK WITH YOU TO FIND THE RIGHT BRA FOR EVERY OCCASION.
- HAVE YOU TRY ON DIFFERENT SIZES AND STYLES FROM A VARIETY OF BRANDS—WHEN IT COMES TO BRAS, THERE'S NO SUCH THING AS A "DEFINITE" SIZE.
- ASK YOU IF YOU'VE LOST OR GAINED WEIGHT SINCE YOUR LAST FITTING OR HAVE BEEN PREGNANT.
- HAVE YOU TRY ON A T-SHIRT, SWEATER, AND BLOUSE OVER A BRA TO GIVE AN IDEA OF HOW IT WILL LOOK UNDER CLOTHES.

Here are some indications of a well-fitted brassiere. First, each breast should fit completely into the cup with no spillage. If it's an underwire style, the underwire should lie flat against your body and not dig into you or stick out in front. Fastened on the second hook (it will stretch as you wear it, so don't buy a bra that only fits on the third set or tightest hook), the band should fit snugly and securely. Don't depend on your straps to do all the hoisting. A good bra supports from the cups and band, not from the straps.

SAME BRASSIERE, YEAR AFTER YEAR?

LZ'S TOUGH LOVE IF YOU WEAR YOUR BRAS FOR YEARS AT A TIME, LET'S TALK. READY? DO. NOT. DO. THAT. ON AVERAGE, BRAS WILL LAST FOR ABOUT NINE MONTHS—MARK YOUR CALENDARS, LADIES! NINE. PERIOD. AFTER THAT, THEY STRETCH OUT, AND ONCE THAT HAPPENS, THEY'RE USELESS AT GIVING YOU THE SUPPORT YOU NEED (WHICH, INCIDENTALLY, IS WHY YOU SHOULDN'T WEAR THE SAME BRA TWO DAYS IN A ROW— GIVE IT A REST BETWEEN WEARINGS OR YOU RISK STRETCHING IT OUT FASTER). WEAR 'EM, LOVE 'EM, THEN THROW 'EM AWAY. AND IF THERE'S ANY DOUBT THAT A BRA NEEDS TO GO, ASK YOURSELF THIS GROWN-UP VARIATION ON YOUR MOTHER'S ADVICE TO ALWAYS WEAR CLEAN UNDERWEAR: IF YOU WOKE UP IN THE EMERGENCY ROOM WEARING A HOSPITAL GOWN, WOULD YOUR FIRST THOUGHT BE THAT YOU WISHED YOU'D WORN A DIFFERENT BRA? I REST MY CASE.

FASHION FOUNDATION #2: PANTIES (AND EVERYTHING ELSE)

When it comes to panties, if you pick the wrong style, not only do you have the dreaded visible panty line (VPL) but you can look like your butt cheeks have multiplied. Two cheeks are enough, yes? Come on, the quadruple butt cheek is not a good look, people!

The always-gorgeous Oprah Winfrey swore off panties years ago and only wears shapewear. If it's good enough for Oprah, it's good enough for you. Having said that, I know that going into the lingerie department at a store can be daunting. The choices are endless (thongs, granny panties, lacy numbers, briefs, boy shorts . . . need I go on?). But take underwear shopping seriously. I beg you to choose the right pieces that complement your style, enhance your body shape, and match your lifestyle. Glamour starts with what's underneath!

Note: For my girls who just rolled their eyes and would never adhere to the Oprah Winfrey school of Panties 101 and who love their thongs, boy-cut boxers, and scanty panties, you're old enough to know that there's a time and place for everything.

THE SHAPE YOU'RE IN

Shapewear can completely resculpt, lift, elevate, smooth out your body, and even take you down a few sizes. It's a party and you're invited. A brief word of warning: Don't wear shapewear that's too tight because it will flatten you out and make your God-given assets look pancake flat.

Here's my list of target areas and the shapewear that will work on them, all at low, medium, and high price points:

THE WAIST

LOW: MIRACLESUIT SHAPEWEAR RIGID FRONT HI-WAIST BRIEF,
APPROXIMATELY $36, WWW.FIGLEAVES.COM

MEDIUM: SPANX UNDIE-TECTABLE HIGH-WAISTED PANTY,
APPROXIMATELY $48–$58, WWW.SPANX.COM

HIGH: JULIE FRANCE CONTOUR HIGH-WAIST BOXER SHAPER,
APPROXIMATELY $68, WWW.CLASSICSHAPEWEAR.COM

THE TUMMY

LOW: SLIM SHAPE WOMEN'S TUMMY SHAPEWEAR CONTROL BRIEFS,
APPROXIMATELY $16, WWW.SEARS.COM

MEDIUM: DUMI SHAPEWEAR TUMMY CONTROL THONG,
APPROXIMATELY $34, WWW.HERROOM.COM

(CONSIDER MAKING EITHER ONE OF THE ABOVE YOUR GO-TO,
EVERYDAY PANTY.)

HIGH: SPANX SUPER HIGHER POWER THIGH AND TUMMY CONTROL
PANTY, APPROXIMATELY $66, WWW.SPANX.COM

THE THIGHS

LOW: SMART & SEXY MEDIUM CONTROL SEAMLESS SHAPEWEAR
THIGH-SLIMMING BIKE SHORTS,
APPROXIMATELY $9, WWW.WALMART.COM

MEDIUM: SKWEEZ COUTURE BY JILL ZARIN SHAPEWEAR FIRM
CONTROL THIGH N MIGHTY WAIST THIGH SKIMMER,
APPROXIMATELY $45, WWW.MACYS.COM

HIGH: AFAP FIRM CONTROL MID-THIGH SHORTS,
APPROXIMATELY $53, WWW.CLASSICSHAPEWEAR.COM

THE CALVES

LOW: HANES WOMEN'S SHAPING CAPRIS,
APPROXIMATELY $13, WWW.HANES.COM

MEDIUM: RAGO SOFT MID CALF LEG SHAPER,
APPROXIMATELY $28, WWW.HERROOM.COM

HIGH: LYSSE SHAPING CAPRI LEGGINGS,
APPROXIMATELY $54, WWW.BARENECESSITIES.COM

THE UPPER ARMS

LOW: YOUR CONTOUR SHORT SLEEVE ARM SHAPER,
APPROXIMATELY $29, WWW.YOURCONTOUR.COM

MEDIUM: YOUR CONTOUR T-SHAPE BODY BRIEFER THONG
ARM CONTROL SHAPEWEAR,
APPROXIMATELY $40, WWW.YOURCONTOUR.COM

HIGH: SPANX ON TOP ELBOW SLEEVE SCOOP NECK TOP,
APPROXIMATELY $98, WWW.HERROOM.COM

And that's not all! As Jennifer Lopez has proven, having a great butt can be quite sexy. If you're looking to smooth out your behind, the thigh slimmers above will do the trick. On the other cheek, if you're looking for a little more junk in your trunk, there are products on the market that will give you that extra bounce. Just as a padded bra can give you extra lift and fullness, padded underwear can do the same thing for your behind! Here are a couple options to try: www.bootypopboutique.com or www.lovemybubbles.com. #bootylicious

FASHION FOUNDATION #3:
JEANS STYLE, THE MASTER CLASS

Let's face it: probably 99 percent of us live in our jeans. It's a fashion staple and I really want to make sure you know how to choose the proper style of jeans.

Ideally, you should aim to have three or four pairs of jeans: a dark-rinse, trouser-cut pair for dressing up; a pair hemmed for flats; and maybe a pair for hanging around the house in (hemmed when needed). You can tweak this formula slightly (for example, straight-leg jeans can be worn with a variety of heel heights because they look good slightly scrunched up with flats, but bootcut jeans need to be hemmed for every heel you're going to wear with them or they'll look all wrong), but in general this formula works for every size.

"I HAVE OFTEN SAID THAT I WISH I HAD INVENTED BLUE JEANS. THE MOST SPECTACULAR, THE MOST PRACTICAL, THE MOST RELAXED AND NONCHALANT. THEY HAVE EXPRESSION, MODESTY, SEX APPEAL, SIMPLICITY — ALL I HOPE FOR IN MY CLOTHES."

—YVES SAINT LAURENT

THE EVERYWOMAN JEANS

The most universally flattering denim cut is the bootleg—it's neither too skinny nor too flared, and it makes sense every time. What you want is a style that's fitted enough (but not sausage-like) through the thigh and knee to show the shape of the leg. The flare of the jeans will make your thighs look slimmer in comparison, and give the impression that your legs are five miles long. Who can argue with that? This type of jeans works on my petite, tall, and full-figure gals too.

JEAN THERAPY

AS I MAY HAVE MENTIONED, I LOVE A BOOTCUT JEAN. DID I MENTION THAT? I'M PRETTY SURE I DID. BUT I KNOW I DID NOT MENTION SPECIFICS. SO, BEHIND DOORS NUMBER ONE, TWO, AND THREE, HERE ARE MY FAVORITE BOOTCUT JEANS AT LOW, MEDIUM, AND HIGH PRICE POINTS.

LOW: OLD NAVY THE SWEETHEART BOOT-CUT JEANS, APPROXIMATELY $30, WWW.OLDNAVY.COM

MEDIUM: THE GAP 1969 LONG & LEAN JEANS, APPROXIMATELY $70, WWW.GAP.COM

HIGH: CITIZENS OF HUMANITY "DITA" BOOTCUT JEANS, APPROXIMATELY $198, WWW.NORDSTROM.COM

THE GOOD, THE BAD, AND THE UGLY

High-waist jeans also need to be approached with caution because they exaggerate the difference between the size of your waist and the size of your hips, making the latter look bigger than they are. Never, under any circumstances, pair this style with flats. Fashion. Disaster. You need all the extra height you can to carry it off.

When it comes to color, I'm a big fan of the dark rinse. It's cool, it's classic, it's slimming, and it always looks right. Also, why not brighten up your wardrobe with colorful jeans? They're fun, they're chic, and everyone's doing it. And yes, even my ladies in their fifties or sixties and older can hone the perfect hue to complement their existing wardrobe.

Yes, I know, you're seeing them everywhere, and it's true, skinny jeans are having a moment. But that doesn't mean it's YOUR moment. I know the lure of trends is strong. If you really want to participate in this one, try the slightly more forgiving straight leg instead. Unless you're supermodel thin and have legs up to the ceiling, skinnies are very tough to pull off—they can make your calves look huge and they can make you look shorter. Why would you ever want to do that?

As we all know, it's the "rear view" that really counts with jeans. Toss a mirror in your bag when you shop just in case the dressing room doesn't want you to have a rear view. I do! To make the most of your rear view, look for a center seam that gives your butt the correct balance of lift and separation (yes, just like your bust). And you can't ignore the importance of pocket size and placement!

THE 20-SECOND RULE

While all of this is good to keep in mind when you're shopping for jeans, the main thing you need to remember is this: If you can't tell in about 20 seconds whether or not the jeans you're trying on look good . . . they don't look good.

And don't think you can go into the fitting room with just one pair and come out with a winner. You need at least three of every style you're trying on: the size you think you are, one bigger, and one smaller. Once you find a pair you like, buy multiples if your budget allows! Finding jeans that fit you well is like finding the pot of gold at the end of the rainbow—what's the chance of it happening again?

GETTING DOWN TO YOUR DETAILS

Warning: In this book, I have vowed to be that brutally honest friend who doesn't tell you what you want to hear—I am here to tell you the truth. Since we're talking about style, not size, I want to help you elevate your style and work your size. There's no nice way to say some of these things, ladies, so just brace yourself.

FLABBY ARMS: If this is an issue for you, stay away from cap and puff sleeves, strapless dresses and tops, and tight-knit sleeves; instead, look for tailored jackets, three-quarter sleeves, cardigans, and dolman sleeves.

MUFFIN TOPS: You have the power to lose your muffin top without losing an ounce. Take off your super low-cut jeans and invest in a pair of mid-rise, dark-rinse, bootcut jeans. Also forbidden: cropped T-shirts and tucking in. What you should be wearing: blousy tops, long tunics, tops with patterns (to keep the eye moving), and structured jackets.

CANKLES: If your ankles are the same size as your calves, you're going to have to be strategic with what you wear. If you like flats, try on long slacks instead of short skirts, and if you're a heel girl, step away from ankle straps and ankle boots, and replace them with d'Orsay pumps, nude pumps, and slingbacks. In the wintertime, pull out your booties and just put on black tights, which will not only keep your legs warm, but will create a longer, leaner silhouette.

BACK FAT: You know what I'm talking about: those wings that pop out underneath your bra that make you look like you've got a spare set of boobs in the back. And yes, that was said with love. To minimize them, first and foremost, find a bra that fits. Once again, be fitted for a bra. And invest in flyaway cardigans, some unconstructed jackets, tailored blazers, and tees with ruched detailing.

TOP FIVE TAKEAWAYS FROM LZ'S FOURTH COMMANDMENT

ONE   IT'S NOT ABOUT BEING A SPECIFIC SIZE; IT'S ABOUT WEARING CLOTHES THAT SUIT YOUR BODY TYPE AND STYLE.

TWO   PROPER TAILORING CAN MAKE INEXPENSIVE CLOTHES LOOK EXPENSIVE AND CUSTOM-MADE.

THREE   GETTING FITTED FOR A BRA ONCE A YEAR WILL SERIOUSLY CHANGE YOUR LIFE, AS WELL AS THE STYLES YOU WEAR, AND THE WAY YOUR CLOTHES LOOK AND FIT.

FOUR   SHAPEWEAR SHOULD BE THE FOUNDATION OF ALMOST EVERY LOOK.

FIVE   THE MOST UNIVERSALLY FLATTERING JEANS ARE DARK DENIM BOOTCUT.

5

THOU SHALT
GO FORTH
AND
ACCESSORIZE

"AT MY AGE, IT'S ALL ABOUT THE ACCESSORIES.

MAJOR BRACELETS, MAJOR PINS, MAJOR NECKLACES,

AND A MAJOR HEARING AID!"

—JOAN RIVERS

■ One of my favorite things to do is to complete every look with just the right accessories. After I've spent hours showing a makeover candidate what to wear and what works, the final step is to accessorize. What I love about accessorizing is that the perfect accessories can take something stylish and make it into a style statement. Like with anything, it's those final details that create that pulled-together look.

Technically, you don't have to wear accessories (the fashion police won't stop you on the street), but I simply don't see why you would deprive yourself of the fun. Let's say, just for kicks, that you're wearing a beautifully cut, little black dress. You think you look pretty good, right? Now, add the perfect metallic evening sandals, an elegant black silk clutch, and chandelier earrings that highlight your face—and voilà! You've taken that look from "it works" to "WOW." And what woman doesn't want that? That is the power of accessories.

Here's another scenario: Let's say you're at the office and it's late and you get a call from the hubby and he wants to take you out after work. Instead of panicking because you have nothing to wear, the great news is that you've read this book and you're already wearing your classic wardrobe pieces. Now all you have to do is change or add accessories and you're ready to move from the workplace right to cocktails, dinner, dancing—the world is your oyster and you look ah-may-zing. The reason why this works? Because from now on, you're going to keep a little accessory kit in your desk drawer or the trunk of your car, including an evening clutch, a pair of sexy heels, and some earrings, all of which are available at prices for any budget (I'm making suggestions in a minute, so hang tight for details).

And what about you stay-at-home moms? You have a tendency to not dress up because you work at . . . wait for it . . . home! You might love your jeans or sweats and have a tendency to rush out for early carpool mornings, but that doesn't mean you don't accessorize. Take a few extra minutes to add one or two items to your daytime basics and you will feel more complete and confident. Try a long oblong scarf around your neck, an oversized pair of sunglasses or a fun pair of earrings, a stylish tote, or a few layered bracelets and you have gone from house mom to starlet mom. It's fun! And don't forget to exchange those gym sneakers for some stylish flats before you head to your errands. I promise it will not only make you look great but you'll also feel great about yourself. Win-win!

"FASHION IS SOCIAL ARMOR, AND POWERED BY THE RIGHT CLOTHES, A WOMAN CAN CONQUER ANYTHING."

—RUBIN SINGER

Beautiful style is all about the details, and these details are the icing on the cake. And in case you're wondering, when I say "accessory," I'm referring to jewelry, scarves, bags, shoes, sunglasses, and eyewear. A big, look-at-me brooch. A dramatic statement necklace. A cocktail ring the size of Montana. Shoes that make you want to strut your stuff. A beautifully made handbag. A scarf that adds a splash of color to your winter coat. Sunglasses that frame your face like a work of art. They're all out there, they're affordable, and they're yours for the taking.

So, let's dive headfirst into the big, beautiful world of accessories, shall we?

LZ'S ACCESSORY NECESSITY #1: SHOES

I love a good shoe and I know you do, too. I've never met a woman who didn't get weak in the knees over pretty shoes. Did you know that the average American woman owns almost 20 pairs of shoes? She doesn't need that many pairs (though with shoes, "need" is a relative term). She has them because she wants them. Shoes make a woman feel sexy. A beautiful shoe sets the tone for your entire outfit . . . or for your entire day! Which is why we should all pause for a moment of silence to absorb these words of wisdom from Christian Dior, one of the greatest designers of the twentieth century: "You can never take too much care over the choice of your shoes. Too many women think that they are unimportant, but the real proof of an elegant woman is what is on her feet." Amen! Ahhh.

THE ALLURE OF A HEEL

When I do a makeover, I love high heels. Heels are seriously God's gift to women. They put the emphasis on your curves and make your legs look approximately 10 miles long. They give you the sexiest walk imaginable. They bring out your inner hotness, which is why no one I've made over has ever regretted going for a heel. It's a win-wow!

"I DON'T KNOW WHO INVENTED HIGH HEELS,
BUT ALL WOMEN OWE HIM A LOT."
—MARILYN MONROE

If you feel like your walk is a bit wobbly in heels, then spend some time practicing around the house. You know the old joke about Carnegie Hall (Q: How do you get to Carnegie Hall? A: Practice, practice, practice.). Walk around in your living room, kitchen, everywhere and on all types of surfaces so you know what it will feel like when you're out and about strutting your stuff. Then, and only then, do those shoes make their public debut.

HEELS AREN'T FOR EVERYONE

YES, IT'S TRUE; I LOVE PUTTING A WOMAN IN A SEXY HIGH HEEL. BUT I'M FULLY AWARE OF THE FACT THAT WHETHER IT'S DUE TO A MEDICAL ISSUE OR COMFORT, SOME WOMEN JUST PREFER TO KEEP THEIR FEET FIRMLY PLANTED ON THE GROUND. JUST KEEP READING FOR LOTS OF OPTIONS TO PUT YOUR BEST FOOT FORWARD, REGARDLESS OF HEEL HEIGHT. IF YOU CAN'T FIND A HIGHER HEEL THAT WORKS FOR YOU, START WITH A KITTEN HEEL (A HEEL SHORTER THAN TWO INCHES) FOR NOW AND KEEP LOOKING. SOMEWHERE OUT THERE IS THE PERFECT HEEL FOR YOU AND IF YOU'RE JUST NEVER GOING TO BE A FAN OF THE HEEL, YOU CAN STILL GET THAT SEXY EDGE WITH THE WEDGE. A WEDGE HEEL WILL STILL GIVE YOU THAT HEIGHT AND ELONGATION, BUT WITH A LITTLE MORE STABILITY IN YOUR STRUT. #OPTIONS

SOLE SUPPORT

IN ORDER TO PROTECT YOUR FAB FOOTSIES, NEVER UNDER-ESTIMATE THE "SOLE" SUPPORT OF INSOLES TO COMFORT, CUSHION, AND PROTECT. THERE ARE LOTS OF VARIATIONS OUT THERE, SUCH AS CUSTOM-MADE INSOLES FROM A DR. SCHOLL'S FOOTMAPPING CENTER (WWW.DRSCHOLLS.COM) OR HANDCRAFTED ORTHOTICS FROM DOCTORINSOLE (WWW.DOCTORINSOLE.COM). THERE ARE ALSO GORGEOUS SHOES THAT ARE DESIGNED WITH COMFORT AND SUPPORT IN MIND. SOME EXAMPLES ARE GEOX (WWW.SHOPGEOX.COM), NATURALIZER (WWW.NATURAL-IZER.COM), AND COLE HAAN PUMPS WITH NIKE TECHNOLOGY (WWW.COLEHAAN.COM). IF YOU TAKE CARE OF YOUR FEET, THEY WILL TAKE CARE OF YOU!

Now, I'm not saying that you need to live in high heels morning, noon, and night like some kind of Stepford wife. If your daily schedule involves a lot of walking, It's smart to plan accordingly and carry a pair of flats, and then before you make your entrance, slip into your heels. Easy. Also, when you're going out on the town, whether it's for dinner or dancing, mentally plan ahead for how long you'll be on your feet, so you can pick the perfect pump.

Sometimes heels just aren't realistic, but that doesn't give you permission to be lazy and put on the same sneakers you wear to the gym. There are plenty of cute, affordable, and comfortable flats that don't involve waffle soles and fluorescent laces. (In fact, take a look at my Fashion Glossary in the back of the book for several fun, flat shoe options.) Remember, you deserve to look good all the time, and looking good starts from the ground up.

LZ'S LIST OF SHOE MUST-HAVES

CLASSIC PUMPS IN BLACK AND NUDE: A pump is your wear-anywhere shoe: work, dinner, family functions, social events. Black goes with everything and Is the most classic of classic shoes. Nude also goes with everything. If you're wearing a dress with several colors in it and you can't decide what to wear on your feet, make your feet disappear with a pair of nude pumps.

A CLASSIC BLACK SLINGBACK: Slightly sexier than the black pump, the black slingback works in more style-conscious offices and is an excellent evening option. It's sexy but ladylike—the Grace Kelly of your shoe wardrobe.

A DRESSY EVENING SANDAL: This is the shoe that you buy because it makes you feel sexy and a little frisky. It's your I-don't-give-a-damn shoe. It should have a high heel and some sort of embellishment. Invest in two—basic black and a metallic.

CUTE FLATS FOR THE WEEKEND: I'm going to keep saying this until you listen: Sneakers are for the gym. Cute flats are for your life. When you're "off duty," you still deserve to look good.

OXFORD LACE-UPS, LOAFERS, OR SHORT BOOTIES FOR DAYTIME, CASUAL EVENINGS, OR WEEKEND WEAR: I like these options for the casual, stylish girls who are paying attention and don't wear sneakers except at the gym. These shoe options offer style and comfort.

CUTE SANDALS FOR THE WEEKEND: This is the summer version of your cute flats—the shoe you're going to wear when you're not at work. You can go trendier and less expensive here, especially because summer shoes tend to get a little trashed by the end of the season and need to be replaced frequently. Some trendy examples include platform wedge sandals, gladiator sandals, and platform sandals, in an assortment of colors, textures, and embellished hardware.

FLIP-FLOPS FOR THE BEACH AND CASUAL SUMMER WEAR: Flip-flops are the perfect summer essential for vacations and easy access to and from the beach. They're fun, they're affordable, and everyone loves them. Flip-flops have recently been elevated to another level of style and are more widely accepted in a variety of settings. In order to flip and not be a flop, always know where you're going and the dress code.

SNEAKERS: For the gym. Enough said.

TOPSIDER: These are great for boating or weekends at the lake.

KNEE-HIGH BLACK BOOTS: These can have a heel or they can be flat—it's up to you. A basic black boot is key for every wardrobe and can be worn in a variety of ways—whether you're clubbing with the girls, pairing them with a basic blazer and jeans, or getting warmed up with black tights for a busy workday or weekend fun. And If you have wider calves, there are plenty of boot options online that are designed just for you. There are even ones that have a stretchy panel, giving you the flexibility you need.

RAIN BOOTS (AKA GALOSHES): Last but not least, don't forget a nice, durable pair of rubber rain boots. Add some personality and go with a fun, fab color or pattern.

LZ'S FINAL "FOOTNOTE": Take good care of your shoes. Invest in shoe trees to help maintain the integrity and shape of the shoe. I do this and my shoes truly do last a lot longer.

IF YOU WIN THE LOTTERY, ADD:

- **ANOTHER PAIR OF PUMPS** BY A TOP DESIGNER, SUCH AS FERRAGAMO, PRADA, CHRISTIAN LOUBOUTIN, OR GUCCI.

- **ANOTHER PAIR OF BOOTS**. IF YOU ALREADY HAVE HIGH-HEEL ONES, MAKE THIS SECOND PAIR FLAT AND VICE VERSA. IF YOU ALREADY HAVE BLACK BOOTS, OPT FOR BROWN.

- **ANKLE BOOTS** (BOOTIE) BECAUSE THEY WORK WITH BOTH PANTS AND SKIRTS.

"SHOES TRANSFORM YOUR BODY LANGUAGE AND ATTITUDE.
THEY LIFT YOU PHYSICALLY AND EMOTIONALLY."
— CHRISTIAN LOUBOUTIN

LZ'S ACCESSORY NECESSITY #2: BAGS

Okay, honey, let's talk about your baggage. No, I don't mean your childhood; I'm talking about your purse. A beautiful bag complements every outfit, but a sloppy one can downgrade your look from fab to drab. While your bag is the one accessory that you don't really "wear," it still has a huge impact on your entire look. Big-time. This is why you have to choose your bag with care and not settle.

WHAT MAKES A BAG FAB

A well-made bag has even stitching with no missing stitches or loose threads, hardware that's solid and dependable (if you close the clasp, the clasp needs to stay closed until you open it again), and good proportions; and it is made of high-quality leather. A good bag should also be suited to your lifestyle. If you're the sort of girl who carries half of her life with her every time she leaves the house, then don't get a dainty little frame bag. If you have to bring files and a laptop home from the office every day, you're going to need a bag that can handle that sort of load—flimsy straps aren't going to cut it. If you're a mom, you need a bag that will hold all your little one's necessities and still keep you looking stylish. The old school diaper bag is a thing of the past and that's where we want it to stay!

So when you're shopping for a bag, keep in mind the specifics of what you need your bag to do:

1. If you often wear a bulky winter coat, try the bag on with the coat.

2. Go ahead and fill it up with the stuff you're going to put in it and see how it looks and feels fully loaded, which can be very different from the way it looks stuffed with tissue paper in the store.

3. Try carrying it over one shoulder first, then the other, then sling it over your arm to see how that feels.

4. Check the clasp to make sure you can easily undo it, including one-handed for those times when you've got your hands full. Also see how fast you can dig out your cell phone or keys from the bottom.

"LUXURY BAGS MAKE YOUR LIFE MORE PLEASANT, MAKE YOU DREAM, GIVE YOU CONFIDENCE, AND SHOW YOUR NEIGHBORS YOU ARE DOING WELL."
—KARL LAGERFELD

THE FOUR BAGS YOU SHOULD HAVE

I believe your "bag wardrobe" should consist of four basic bags.

1. A WORK BAG: Make sure it's a classic shape, can hold your laptop or tablet or whatever else you need, and is a neutral color like black or dark brown—other colors just don't have staying power. A hobo, a structured tote, or a shoulder bag are all good work options. (Be sure to flip to the Fashion Glossary in the back to see illustrations and definitions for each of these types of bags.) #WorkIt

PRICE: This is probably the bag you'll spend the most money on, but don't max out your credit card before checking out off-price retailers like Marshall's (www.marshallsonline.com) and T.J. Maxx (www.tjmaxx.com). These are two of my favorite off-price retailers, where you can save 20 to 60 percent off department store prices. The secret is to check their stores often because they get new shipments of merchandise every day and if you're one of those fancy girls who loves your designer labels, this is the place to get them. You can also check out eBay and other Internet sources. Secondhand desginer bags are often available at incredible prices. If you find one you love, take it to your favorite shoe repair and have them recondition it to perfection.

SHOW YOU CARE: HOW TO LOOK AFTER YOUR BAGS

YOUR BAGS NEED SOME TLC IN ORDER TO STAY LOOKING GREAT FOR YEARS TO COME. STORE THEM UPRIGHT IN A WELL-VENTILATED SPACE, AND DON'T CROWD THEM IF YOU CAN AVOID IT. IF YOUR BAG CAME WITH A DUST BAG, USE IT! WHATEVER YOU DO, DON'T HANG A BAG BY ITS STRAPS—THIS WILL STRETCH THEM OUT AND PUT A LOT OF STRESS ON THE STITCHING. AND WHEN A REPAIR NEEDS TO BE DONE, TAKE YOUR BAG TO THE SHOEMAKER. THEY CAN REPLACE ZIPPERS, STITCH UP SEAMS, FIX HARDWARE, AND CONDITION LEATHER. SERIOUSLY, THESE GUYS CAN DO PRACTICALLY ANYTHING!

ALSO, AS MY GREEK GODDESS OF A SISTER-IN-LAW, MARIA, SAYS, YOU SHOULD NEVER PUT YOUR HANDBAG ON THE FLOOR BECAUSE WHEN YOU DO, ALL YOUR MONEY MAY RUN OUT OF IT. OH, SIDE NOTE—I LOVE THIS GIRL! NOT ONLY DID SHE GIVE ME MY DELICIOUS NEPHEWS, ALEXANDER AND CHRISTIAN, BUT SHE TRULY IS ONE OF THE BEST THINGS THAT'S EVER HAPPENED TO OUR FAMILY. ON TOP OF ALL THAT, SHE IS AN AMAZING HANDBAG DESIGNER. CHECK OUT HER UNIQUE PIECES AT WWW.MANDONIA.COM. #FAMILY

BY DESIGN: ARE DESIGNER BAGS REALLY WORTH IT?

LIKE A BIG ROCK ON YOUR FINGER, A DESIGNER BAG IS AN UNMISTAK-ABLE STATUS ITEM. FOR SOME WOMEN, IT'S AN INSTANT CONFIDENCE BOOSTER. OTHER WOMEN LOOK AT THE PRICE TAG AND THINK NO WAY, NOT NOW, NO HOW! MY VIEW IS THAT IF YOU DO DECIDE TO SPLURGE ON A BIG-TICKET, BIG-NAME DESIGNER BAG, MAKE SURE IT'S A CLASSIC STYLE AND COLOR THAT YOU'LL CARRY FOR YEARS. YOU DO NOT WANT TO SPEND BIG BUCKS ON A BAG THAT'S GOING TO BE OUT OF STYLE IN LESS THAN SIX MONTHS. THAT IS CALLED IMPULSE SHOPPING, WHICH THEN TRANSITIONS TO BUYER'S REMORSE THAT YOU WILL NEVER FORGET; AND EVERY TIME YOU LOOK AT THAT BAG, YOU'LL THINK OF THE MONEY YOU SPENT AND WASTED ON SOMETHING THAT HAS COME AND GONE.

2. A BIG BAG THAT DOUBLES AS AN OVERNIGHT BAG: This is the bag you'll use for schlepping everything: kids' stuff, clothing, toiletries, extras, et cetera. Your big bag doesn't need to be as formal as your work bag, but it should still be a good-quality bag. Some good examples are an oversized satchel or chic duffel bag.

3. A FUN BAG FOR THE WEEKENDS: On the weekends, just like you, your bag needs some time off. You don't need to spend as much on a weekend bag, so this is where you can get a bit trendier, more colorful, and have some fun. This is the bag you're going to carry if you're meeting your girlfriends for brunch or running some errands. You can let your personality shine with this bag and really celebrate your inner Carrie Bradshaw . . . or Samantha, Charlotte, Miranda, you pick the girl. Think fun, fancy, feminine.

4. A BASIC BLACK CLUTCH FOR EVENINGS: There's nothing that says style and class in the evenings better than a basic black clutch. It can be leather, satin, velvet, or beaded. I like clutches because they have a subtle retro feel (check out consignment and antique stores), they go with everything, and their clean, simple lines don't fight your overall look. And as you know, I want all your clothes to get along, people!

IF YOU WIN THE LOTTERY, ADD:

- **A TOP DESIGNER BAG**—IT'S CONSIDERED WEARABLE ART. JUST DON'T LET THE DESIGNER'S NAME OR LOGO OVERPOWER THE BAG. A SUBTLE LOGO IS STYLISH, A BRASH LOGO SCREAMS "TRIED TOO HARD."

- **A SUMMER WORK BAG** IN A LIGHTER LEATHER, SUCH AS BEIGE OR TAN (A LEATHER-TRIMMED CANVAS IS A SUMMER CLASSIC THAT ALWAYS LOOKS GOOD).

- **A STRAW TOTE** THAT DOUBLES AS YOUR FUN BAG DURING THE SUMMER MONTHS.

- **A BEACH BAG**—SUCH AS A CANVAS BAG THAT MAKES YOU FEEL LIKE YOU'RE ON VACATION.

- **A SECOND EVENING CLUTCH**—IF YOUR FIRST ONE IS PLAIN, GET AN EMBELLISHED ONE.

LZ'S ACCESSORY NECESSITY #3: JEWELRY

Whether you wear major carats or fabulous fakes (and I'd like to point out that no less than Coco Chanel herself was a huge fan of costume jewelry), you need to discover the wonderful world of jewelry. I really believe that every woman should have a basic jewelry inventory that is anchored by classic pieces.

THE JEWELRY CHECKLIST

Here are the basic pieces you need in your jewelry wardrobe.

EARRINGS

HOOPS: Get these in small, medium, and large. You can find them for practically nothing at your local department store or places like Claire's (www.claires.com) or Accessorize (www.accessorize.com). When it comes to your choice of metal, gold, silver, and gunmetal all work, but I suggest you stick with one color per outfit.

DIAMOND STUDS: Real if you can; if not, faux can also be fab. You don't want to go too big or too small here. Go for something that you can see, but not from 20 feet away. I love these with everything from jeans to cocktail dresses.

PEARL STUDS: Again, real and fake are equally good; it's the effect we're interested in, kids. They should be big enough to be seen but not so big that it looks like marshmallows are attacking your ears.

YOUR WILD-CARD OPTIONS: A great pair of fancy drop earrings, such as a chandelier or teardrop . . . and whatever you choose, make them festive.

NO PIERCING? NO PROBLEM!

IF YOU DON'T HAVE PIERCED EARS, NEVER FEAR. EARRING CONVERTERS ARE HERE! THEY TURN POST EARRINGS INTO CLIP EARRINGS IN NO TIME AT ALL. I FOUND SOME FOR $10 AT WWW.BLAIR.COM.

NECKLACES

CHAINS: Stick with your chosen metal and get them in three lengths—one that hits just below the collar, one that's a little longer and you can wear with more revealing tops, and one that reaches between your bra band and your belly button. And while we're on the subject of chains, let's talk charms. Charms are a trend I approve of because they're actually a classic that has made a resurgence. They're a great way to personalize a chain, especially when you wear a few of them at a time and they have some sort of special meaning to you, such as your initials and/or your favorite symbols.

PEARLS: Every woman needs pearls (again, real or faux). Get them in different lengths, just as you do your metal chains. A choker to fill in the neckline of a button-down (FYI, this a fabulous way to feminize a menswear staple), opera length to wear outside a party dress, and something in between. Pearls look great when you pile them on, so feel free to layer them. Case in point: If you want to add some instant glamour, layer on all of your pearl necklaces over a plain black pullover. It's definitly chic. Just don't add pearl earrings and a pearl bracelet or you'll look like you're on your way to audition for an eighties sitcom.

YOUR WILD-CARD OPTIONS: When you have a little extra cash to spend, have some fun with your accessories and make a statement with a big, bold necklace; it can be bib style; a giant pendant; big, graduated beads—whatever it is, make it count.

RINGS

A COCKTAIL RING: It always looks good and is the perfect accessory for a night out, weekends, and dressy events. Check out Maurices (www.maurices.com) for big, beautiful baubles that start as low as $8 apiece.

BRACELETS

CUFFS: When it comes to bracelets, I practice cuff love, but I'm monogamous. One cuff at a time, ladies. I'm not a fan of the double-cuff. This is one of those times when symmetry is not the way to go.

BANGLES: A stack of metallic bangles is not only incredibly versatile, it's extremely chic. Again, stick with your chosen metal.

BRING ON THE OTHER BRACELETS: Whether plastic, wooden, beaded, or acrylic, there's a big bracelet buffet out there. It's a fun way to accessorize and add to your look. Try www.overstock.com.

WATCHES

They tell the time, but watches also make a statement and complement your outfit. The watch you choose is definitely a personal choice and just as important as the other accessories you wear with each look.

IF YOU WIN THE LOTTERY, ADD:

- A HIGH-END EUROPEAN WATCH SUCH AS BVLGARI, CHOPARD, OR CARTIER.
- A UNIQUE VINTAGE PENDANT. CHECK OUT WWW.BLUENILE.COM.
- GOLD CHARMS. CHECK OUT WWW.HELENFICALORA.COM.
- A DIAMOND SOLITAIRE PENDANT AND STUDS. CHECK OUT WWW.TIFFANY.COM.

CHOOSING THE RIGHT JEWELRY FOR YOUR TOP

I see it all the time: women wearing perfectly lovely jewelry, but ruining the look by pairing the wrong tops with it. Here are my simple rules for putting the right jewelry with the right tops.

BOATNECK: This top runs in an almost straight line from shoulder to shoulder, is a classic, and rightly so. But it's notoriously tricky to accessorize because it visually cuts you off at the neck. Counteract this effect by layering on long multi-strand necklaces that create the illusion of a longer torso.

V-NECK: With the V-neck, you want to work with that sexy V-shaped slice of exposed skin. Either choose a statement necklace that fits inside the chest real estate or add length to the V shape by choosing a longer necklace that draws the eye downward.

SCOOP NECK: This is the easiest neckline to accessorize. Basically, you can wear any necklace you like and any length, as long as it doesn't hit the bottom of the scoop.

STRAPLESS: The strapless neckline was designed to showcase a lot of skin. Make the most of this with a necklace that drops above or slightly lower than just under the collarbone. Focus on the earrings, the bracelets, and the ring.

CREWNECK: This is that higher, round neck that you find on a T shirt or sweater, and it's best to go with no necklace at all. Instead, your accessory should be a cuff bracelet, stacked bangles, or a cocktail ring.

RULE ALERT: Whatever necklace you choose, remember my Rule of Opposites: The bigger the necklace, the smaller the earrings, and vice versa. The big/small rule keeps you beautifully balanced.

CHOOSING THE RIGHT JEWELRY FOR YOUR FACE

Now that we've covered how to choose the right jewelry for various tops, it's time to address how to choose jewelry that will complement the natural shape of your face. Here are some quick guidelines to help pick the right jewelry for your face.

OVAL-SHAPED FACE: Oval faces are widest across the temples and forehead.

CELEBRITIES: Jennifer Aniston and Kristen Stewart

Women with an oval-shaped face can basically get away with anything when it comes to earrings and necklaces.

PEAR-SHAPED FACE: In a pear-shaped or triangular-shaped face, the chin and jaw are narrow, with wider cheeks and a forehead that is even wider.

CELEBRITY: Jodi Foster

From opera-length necklaces to longer earrings, the length elongates the face and creates needed balance.

HEART-SHAPED FACE: Similar to a diamond-shaped face. The jawline is narrow and the chin is pointed.

CELEBRITIES: Scarlett Johansson and Jennifer Love Hewitt

For a heart-shaped face, shorter necklaces work best because they balance out the thin chin by adding some bulk. Tiny studs and hoop earrings work. You can also try teardrop- or pyramid-style earrings because they add some width around the chin.

SQUARE-SHAPED FACES: Wide jawline and forehead. Oblong/rectangular-shaped faces are similar, just slightly longer and narrower.

CELEBRITIES: Keira Knightley and Demi Moore

Longer necklaces work best. In regards to earrings, studs work beautifully. You can also use earrings with round, angular shapes that soften the strong features.

ROUND-SHAPED FACES: Round-shaped faces are widest at the cheekbones and the circular shape of the face is just as wide as it is long.

CELEBRITIES: Cameron Diaz and Penelope Cruz

Longer necklaces are always a good option. They add length to the face and draw the eyes downward. Long, teardrop, and dangling earrings work best.

A FINISHING TOUCH

Before we leave the glamorous world of jewelry, I'm going to throw out a suggestion: brooches. You can use them to:

- CREATE A PENDANT FOR YOUR PEARL NECKLACE— JUST CLIP ON AND GO.

- FASTEN A SCARF OR BUTTON-LESS CARDIGAN.

- SERVE AS A BELT BUCKLE.

- CLIP TO A HAIRPIN AND USE AS A HAIR ACCESSORY (I LOVE THIS IN AN UPDO FOR EVENING).

- FASTEN TO A LENGTH OF RIBBON TO MAKE A BRACELET OR CHOKER NECKLACE.

- GROUP SEVERAL PINS WITH THE SAME THEME TOGETHER ON A JACKET LAPEL.

The best brooches are vintage because the quality and workmanship on older pieces tend to be better. You can find great vintage brooches in flea markets and thrift shops or in your grandma's jewelry box. Just make sure you ask nicely before you take anything, and write a sweet thank-you note. #ILoveYouGrandma

LZ'S ACCESSORY NECESSITY #4: GLASSES AND SUNGLASSES

Ladies, gone are the days when glasses were a no-fun, utilitarian piece of hardware strictly meant to improve your vision. If you've never actually thought of your glasses as an accessory before, well, listen up because I'm determined to show you just how beautifully a pair of glasses can complement your overall look. Dorothy Parker, famed satirist, was a funny, funny lady and she'll always be remembered for her wit and wisecracks. Her famous "Men don't make passes at girls who wear glasses" quip dates back to the 1920s, when women's choices in eyewear were essentially "ugly" or "uglier." Today, you can don a pair of cute, chic frames that draw the eye upward and show that you've got a fun sense of style.

> "DO NOT ALLOW PEOPLE TO DIM YOUR SHINE BECAUSE THEY ARE BLINDED.
> TELL THEM TO PUT ON SOME SUNGLASSES."
> —LADY GAGA

In finding the perfect frames for you, I suggest that you shop around for your frames because prices vary quite a bit from shop to shop and designer to designer. I'm always surprised when someone has pulled an entire look together and the only thing that doesn't work is their frames. So when The Vision Council (www.thevisioncouncil.org) approached me to work with them, I discovered that we share the same philosophy for choosing the perfect eyewear. It was a 20/20 match made in eyewear heaven and I love working with them.

WHERE TO GET YOUR GLASSES

Eyewear is so en vogue. The style options are endless and the huge price range will accommodate every budget. Whatever your eyewear needs (readers, everyday glasses, or sunglasses) are and whatever you can afford, here is a selection of eyewear websites that will help you see more clearly:

- **READERS.COM**: WWW.READERS.COM
- **EYEBOBS**: WWW.EYEBOBS.COM
- **WARBY PARKER**: WWW.WARBYPARKER.COM
- **FOSTER GRANT**: WWW.FOSTERGRANT.COM
- **PEEPERSPECS**: WWW.PEEPERSPECS.COM

LZ FASHION TIP: Also, don't toss out your old frames. You can have new lenses added or change a pair of regular glasses to sunglasses, or vice versa, to have many more options. Believe it or not, Costco (www.costco.com) will put new lenses in your old frames at a great price while you're building your eyewear wardrobe.

SUNGLASSES ALERT

DID YOU KNOW THAT 40 PERCENT OF ADULTS DON'T WEAR SUNGLASSES, WHICH MEANS THEY ARE AT HIGHER RISK FOR CATARACTS, MACULAR DEGENERATION, AND—WAIT FOR IT—WRINKLES. (#UGH) WHEN BUYING SUNGLASSES, REMEMBER THAT YOU WANT FRAMES THAT HAVE BROAD SPECTRUM UV PROTECTION. THE RIGHT PAIR OF SUNGLASSES NOT ONLY MAKES YOU LOOK AWESOME BUT PROTECTS YOUR EYES TOO. TWO FOR ONE, WHY WOULDN'T YOU HAVE SEVERAL PAIRS: SOME FOR YOUR CAR, YOUR PURSE, YOUR OFFICE—IF YOU'RE ANYTHING LIKE ME, YOU HAVE A TENDENCY TO MISPLACE FRAMES. THE BOTTOM LINE IS FASHION, FUNCTION, AND FUN!

LZ'S FRAMED TO PERFECTION:
EYEWEAR FOR EVERY FACE SHAPE

IT'S ALSO IMPORTANT TO CHOOSE FRAMES THAT:

- Fit comfortably on the face.
- Don't press against your head or slide down your nose or sit on your cheeks.
- Keep your eyes in the center of the lenses (if not, then the frame is too wide).
- Sit at a 90-degree angle to your face.
- Have temples long enough to fit comfortably behind your ears.

MADE IN THE SHADE

AVIATOR	WAYFARER	RECTANGULAR	WRAP AROUND

BUTTERFLY	ROUND	CAT EYE	WIRE RIMMED

RIMLESS	OVERSIZED	JACKIE O	GOGGLE

SHAPE IT UP:
PICK THE RIGHT FRAME FOR YOUR FACE

You've been framed! Above, you'll see my lovely list of beautiful frames for your eyewear—now, let's talk about how to choose the right frames for your face. I don't want you to be a fashion disaster by wearing a pair of glasses that looks ridiculous on you. (You can even find out more, including styles and designer selections, at www.eyecessorize.com.)

HEART-SHAPED FACE

CELEBRITIES: Reese Witherspoon, Jennifer Garner

GOAL: Broaden appearance of the chin and minimize width of forehead

FRAME SUGGESTIONS: Aviator, butterfly, rimless, or semi-rimless

WHAT TO AVOID:

- Wide frames with straight lines
- Horizontal lines and pointed bottoms
- Oversized frames that extend past the temples
- Overly embellished frames

ROUND FACE

CELEBRITIES: Drew Barrymore, Kelly Clarkson

GOAL: Play down fullness of a round face

FRAME SUGGESTIONS: Rectangles or squares, wayfarers, sporty or squared-off retro styles

WHAT TO AVOID:

- Rounded frames or lenses

SQUARE FACE

CELEBRITIES: Nicole Kidman, Sandra Bullock

GOAL: Soften and balance out a strong jawline; make face appear longer

FRAME SUGGESTIONS: Round, oval Jackie O styles, cat eye

WHAT TO AVOID:

- Boxy and angular frames
- Frames that are flat on the bottom

OVAL FACE

CELEBRITIES: Rihanna, Jessica Alba

GOAL: Keep the natural balance of the oval

FRAME SUGGESTIONS: Lucky you! Any frame shape looks beautiful on you. Of course, try them on and make sure you like them, but for the most part, you truly have the pick of the litter.

WHAT TO AVOID:

- Nothing!

OBLONG FACE

CELEBRITIES: Sarah Jessica Parker, Angelina Jolie

GOAL: Minimize length of the face; add a little width and shorten the length

FRAME SUGGESTIONS: Oversized and wrap arounds

WHAT TO AVOID:

- Narrow or short frames

THE RIGHT GLASSES FOR YOUR SKIN TONE

The color of your glasses frames should go well with your skin tone. Here's a simple guide to complementing your natural skin tone with the color of your glasses:

- **WARMER SKIN TONES**: Your skin has more color, so you gravitate toward the golden colors in clothes. You should wear yellow-based colors, and also lighter shades of plastics like ivory and off-white.

- **COOL SKIN TONES**: Your skin is fair and you look best with softer colors next to your face and silver accessories. You should wear silvers, grays, and blues.

- Black and white shades look great on blondes, but red adds a hint of drama.

- If your skin has pink undertones, avoid reds as they can make you look pinker.

- If your skin is pale or has yellow undertones, certain yellowy tortoises can make skin look sallow.

LZ'S ACCESSORY NECESSITY #5: SCARVES

Scarves are such an easy and inexpensive way to switch up a look. For example, if you're wearing your classic two-piece black pants suit and a crisp white dress shirt that I told you to buy, layer on an exotic print scarf and you've taken that look from "work" to "wow."

When I do makeovers, I'm often asked for ideas on how to accessorize in fresh ways. With a scarf, you've got so many options. When it comes to finding an assortment of ways to "get your scarf on," go on Google or check out www.ehow.com. Wrap one in your hair, layer one around your neck for a lush turtleneck effect, use one as a belt, or tie it around the handle of your bag. The options are endless.

IF YOU WIN THE LOTTERY, ADD:

- A SILK SQUARE SCARF IN A CLASSIC PATTERN. AN HERMÉS SCARF IS SUCH A STATEMENT PIECE. IT GIVES YOU "STATUS" STYLE. #HERMES
- A LONG CASHMERE SCARF IN TRUFFLE BROWN, BORDEAUX, IVORY, OR RUBY RED.

LZ'S ACCESSORY NECESSITY #6: BELTS

Adding a belt to a pair of pants means that you've gone that extra step of choosing something that complements and finishes what you're wearing. Try it; even with a pair of jeans, a belt creates that instant pulled-together look. And there is nothing better at defining a waist. Worn with a sheath dress, as Michelle Obama likes to do, a belt gives the eye a focal point and emphasizes your curves. Ditto over a long cardigan—you get the extra layer without losing your waist. Because a waist is a terrible thing to waste. (Ha-ha—I made another fashion funny!) Some blazers and winter coats look more expensive by adding a belt. #InstaGlam

You don't have to dedicate an entire wall of your closet to your belt collection; you're perfectly fine keeping a small basic belt inventory. One-inch-wide leather belts in black, navy, and brown will work with almost anything. For the buckle, keep it in the same family as the metal you've chosen for your jewelry. For a little extra something over a dress or blouse-and-skirt combo, I like a three-inch-wide belt in black leather or black patent leather. This gives you a sexy retro look that is very old Hollywood. And if you want to add some more belts to your collection, here are some ideas:

- AN ANIMAL PRINT BELT
- A RED LEATHER BELT
- A GROSGRAIN RIBBON BELT IN A FUN COLOR FOR SUMMER
- A POLKA DOT OR CHECK PATTERNED BELT FOR A TOUCH OF WHIMSY
- A PEARL AND GOLD CHAIN BELT FOR THAT COCO CHANEL TOUCH

"I ADORE WEARING GEMS, BUT NOT BECAUSE THEY ARE MINE. YOU CAN'T POSSESS RADIANCE, YOU CAN ONLY ADMIRE IT."

—ELIZABETH TAYLOR

TOP FIVE TAKEAWAYS FROM LZ'S FIFTH COMMANDMENT

ONE ACCESSORIES WILL ALWAYS SHOWCASE YOUR PERSONALITY AND EXPRESS YOUR MOOD FOR THE DAY.

TWO A NUDE PUMP MAKES YOUR LEGS LOOK A MILE LONG AND GOES WITH ALMOST ANYTHING.

THREE IF YOUR BUDGET ALLOWS, INVEST IN A SMALL INVENTORY OF CLASSIC JEWELRY PIECES, SUCH AS DIAMOND AND PEARL STUDS.

FOUR TAKE CARE OF YOUR SHOES AND BAGS AND THEY'LL RETURN THE FAVOR BY LASTING FOR YEARS.

FIVE SCARVES IN TRENDY COLORS LET YOU UPDATE YOUR LOOK WITHOUT BLOWING YOUR BUDGET.

6 | THOU SHALT
CREATE
YOUR OWN
STAR STYLE

"FASHIONS FADE, STYLE IS ETERNAL."

—YVES SAINT LAURENT

■ When I do my makeovers, a lot of my women tell me they want to look like the stars they see on the Hollywood red carpets and at the big award shows. Allow me to give you a little wake-up call here, ladies. Red-carpet looks are meant for the red carpet. Period. Even the most stunning celebrities don't look like that when they're not working the red. Take it from me; I've seen them up close and personal, so I ought to know.

Secondly, just because a celeb is rocking a certain look doesn't automatically mean that you could (or should) rock it too. Don't think "in style," think "MY style." Did you catch that? Discovering your own personal style is seriously the KEY to looking your best at all times. That's what the stars you see on TV have discovered: their own style.

"THE FASHIONABLE WOMAN WEARS CLOTHES.
THE CLOTHES DON'T WEAR HER."
—MARY QUANT

To know your own style, you've got to be willing to put in some work. Women who have incredible personal style are really skilled at thinking in terms of the "big picture." They pay attention to line, silhouette, color, and proportion. Furthermore, they know what's in their closets at any given time, how it all works together, and which pieces are missing.

But you never see the work that goes into their overall elegance because they make it look effortless. And this is largely because they follow my three rules of great style:

LZ'S 3 RULES OF GREAT PERSONAL STYLE

1. **DETAILS ARE KEY.** Great style means that you don't just throw on all of your favorite pieces and trust they'll work together. It means advance planning to make the most of every element of each piece you put on.

2. **KNOW YOURSELF AND WHAT SUITS YOU.** When you shop, keep in mind your body, lifestyle, budget, and needs. Don't try to fool yourself because that never works.

3. **DRESS FOR YOUR AGE.** I can't stress this enough. You can have the body of a 25-year-old and the face of a 30-year old, but if you are 45, you have no business dressing like your teenage daughter. These words come from a place of love and exprience, ladies.

WHO'S YOUR FASHION ICON?

Your fashion icon is someone whose personal style speaks to you. There are dozens of these glorious ladies and they span all decades, ages, and styles. Why not channel some of their chic, unique style into your own wardrobe? After all, trends have been set, collections have been inspired, and no one said we couldn't steal from them! Chances are, if you admire someone's overall look, it speaks to you—and if it speaks, listen!

"FASHION IS WHAT YOU'RE OFFERED FOUR TIMES A YEAR
BY DESIGNERS. AND STYLE IS WHAT YOU CHOOSE."
—LAUREN HUTTON

CLASSIC, YES. BORING, NO.

Now, please note: I'm not telling you to forget all the advice I've given you about building a classic wardrobe. I am all about the classics, and you should be too! But classic doesn't mean cookie-cutter. Once you've got the basics, you can start to personalize—and that's where your style icon comes in.

To get you into the fashion icon mindset, I've put together a selection of styles and the iconic women who embody each one. For each style, I've listed a few pieces of clothing and accessories that you can add to your basics to achieve the look. Don't forget to have fun!

"CLOTHES MEAN NOTHING UNTIL SOMEONE LIVES IN THEM."
MARC JACOBS

LZ'S GUIDE TO FINDING YOUR PERFECT FASHION ICON

Grab a pen, because you're going to want to take notes. Fashion class is now in session! I've put together a list of the women who have made fashion hearts go pitter patter and set major trends over the last half century. Study them, learn their ways, and copy as much as you can—this is one class where copying is encouraged. (FYI—there are hundreds, maybe thousands, of photos of all of these women online, so check those out for extra inspiration and add them to your closet style board.)

THE ALL-AMERICAN

The most trend-proof and enduring of looks, All-American style stems from our collective fascination with the East Coast upper-class lifestyle. Think Ralph Lauren ads and old photos of the Kennedys. It's a clean-cut blend of menswear-inspired and feminine pieces that stress good cuts, function, and clean lines over showy details.

IF THIS IS THE LOOK YOU'RE AFTER, ADD THESE PIECES TO YOUR BASICS:

- LARGE, OVERSIZED FRAMES
- THE PERFECT WHITE TAILORED SHIRT
- A PEA COAT IN BLACK OR NAVY
- HEELED LOAFERS
- CRISP WHITE JEANS
- A CAMEL WOOL BLAZER
- A CANVAS AND LEATHER HOBO BAG

THE CLASSIC ALL-AMERICAN: JACKIE KENNEDY ONASSIS

WHO SHE IS: The First Lady of the United States, of course, but also an accomplished equestrienne, a patron of the arts, a lover of French culture, and an established and celebrated book editor.

WHY SHE'S AN ICON: As one of the youngest First Ladies ever, Jackie favored clean-lined suits and shift dresses in vibrant hues, low-heeled pumps, and the pillbox hat, which she brought into vogue. In her post-White House life, she was known for her oversized sunglasses, sweater-and-jeans ensembles, tailored pants suits, and silk Hermès head scarves. Her bouffant hair was a style signature.

"FEW WOMEN IN HISTORY HAVE CAPTURED THE IMAGINATION
THE WAY SHE DID, AND IT WAS JACKIE'S COURAGE AND
GRACE THAT HAVE MADE HER IMAGE AN ENDURING ONE.
SHE WAS AN ORIGINAL, AN ICON."
—VALENTINO

THE GAMINE

("Gamine," FYI, is French for a playful, mischievous girl. In plain old English, it refers to an elegant tomboy.)

The Gamine mixes French chic with American simplicity—she's a tomboy but in the most refined, chic way imaginable. The Gamine's clothes are simple and timeless but put together in relaxed and unexpected ways.

IF THIS IS THE LOOK YOU'RE AFTER, ADD THESE PIECES TO YOUR BASICS.

- BLACK BALLET FLATS
- A BLACK OR NAVY TRENCH COAT
- CAPRI PANTS
- A STRIPED, BOATNECK KNIT SWEATER
- DIAMOND OR PEARL STUDS
- THE CLASSIC WHITE TAILORED SHIRT WORN OUT, NOT TUCKED IN

THE CLASSIC GAMINE: AUDREY HEPBURN

WHO SHE IS: First a ballet dancer and then an Academy Award®-winning actress, Audrey Hepburn was also widely recognized for her humanitarian work with UNICEF, and was awarded the Presidential Medal of Freedom for her work with the United Nations.

WHY SHE'S AN ICON: In an age when the blond bombshell (think Marilyn Monroe and Jayne Mansfield) reigned supreme, Audrey Hepburn single-handedly made it chic to be a willowy brunette. Whether she was wearing her favorite Capri pants and a man's shirt or an elegant Givenchy evening gown, her look was clean and effortlessly elegant.

> "THE IMPRINT OF MISS HEPBURN IS ABSOLUTELY, TOTALLY PRESENT.
> LIKE IT OR NOT, SHE WILL BE THE MOST IMPORTANT LOOK
> OF THE TWENTIETH CENTURY."
> —MANOLO BLAHNIK

THE LADY

Sophisticated and feminine, the Lady is the kind of woman who was born to dress up. Even in jeans, she has that something extra—she looks elegant and put together. She's always well groomed, and she adores beautiful shoes, a gorgeous handbag, and a figure-defining dress.

IF THIS IS THE LOOK YOU'RE AFTER, ADD THESE PIECES TO YOUR BASICS:

- A STRUCTURED, SQUARE-SHAPED, DARK LEATHER HANDBAG IN EITHER BASIC BLACK OR RICH TRUFFLE BROWN
- A TAILORED COAT IN EITHER BLACK, NAVY, OR BROWN
- A MULTICOLOR SQUARE SILK SCARF
- A VINTAGE-INSPIRED, '50S OR '60S TAILORED DRESS
- A CLASSIC BLACK PUMP

THE CLASSIC LADY: GRACE KELLY

WHO SHE IS: Still one of Hollywood's most beloved actresses even today, Grace Kelly was one of Alfred Hitchcock's blonde muses, and an Academy Award®-winning actress. She went from Hollywood royalty to actual royalty when she married Prince Rainier of Monaco in 1956 in one of the most fairy-tale-like weddings ever celebrated.

WHY SHE'S AN ICON: Already known for her exquisite taste before her marriage, Grace Kelly became a fashion icon when she was frequently photographed carrying an Hermès handbag while trying to conceal her first pregnancy from the press. Renamed the "Kelly," it's one of the chicest bags you'll ever see—which is why even on eBay, it goes for four figures.

"IT WASN'T A STYLE. IT WAS HER STYLE, HER CARRIAGE AS A PERSONA, HER PERSONALITY STYLE, THE WAY SHE CARRIED HERSELF, WHICH WAS COMPATIBLE AND COMPLETELY IN LINE WITH THE WAY SHE DRESSED. IT MADE IT A VERY CLEAR STORY. THE OUTLINES WERE CLEAR LINES. THAT WOMAN WAS NOT TRYING TO DRESS UP IN A FASHIONABLE OR TRENDY WAY. HER LOOK ALWAYS HAD AN ARISTOCRATIC EDGE."

—PATRICIA FIELD, COSTUMER

THE PRINCESS

If I were to sum up the Princess in three words, they would be: polished, luxurious, and refined. The Princess loves a sophisticated look that celebrates fashion without ever being a slave to it—she'll mix designer pieces with less expensive ones. Her hallmarks are old-fashioned good taste and an understated opulence.

IF THIS IS THE LOOK YOU'RE AFTER, ADD THESE PIECES TO YOUR BASICS:

- A JEWEL-TONE FITTED DRESS
- AN ELEGANT SILK BLOUSE IN EITHER IVORY, RAVISHING RED, OR ROYAL BLUE
- A SIGNATURE BROOCH, EITHER VINTAGE OR AN EXPENSIVE REPRODUCTION
- A CLASSIC CHANEL-STYLE BOUCLE JACKET
- PEARL STUDS AND CHOKER LENGTH NECKLACE
- A BLACK, PATENT LEATHER QUILTED TOTE

THE CLASSIC PRINCESS: LADY DIANA SPENCER

WHO SHE IS: Upon her marriage to Prince Charles in 1981, 20-year-old Lady Diana Spencer instantly became one of the most closely watched women on the planet. She was a supporter of the American Red Cross's landmine campaign and AIDS-related charities, and she broke with royal tradition by giving her children a less rigid upbringing. Most notably, she spoke publicly of her personal struggles and exposed herself on a global level, thereby making herself relatable to the rest of the world.

WHY SHE'S AN ICON: During her marriage, Diana was extremely conventional when it came to style. But she emerged as a confident, sexy woman after her divorce. In fact, the dress she wore for her first appearance after Charles's public acknowledgement of his infidelities set the stage for what was to come: a slinky black cocktail dress with a plunging neckline that showcased her killer figure and great legs. Va-va-VOOM.

"SHE INTRIGUED THE WORLD WITH HER BLEND OF INTOXICATING SOPHISTICATION AND HER SINCERE TOUCH."

—CHARLES SPENCER, EARL SPENCER, DIANA'S BROTHER

THE ROCK STAR

Is there a woman out there who hasn't wanted to look like a rock star, even if it was only for a little while? Don't lie to me, girls, I can see you!

The Rock Star sets the stage for a look that is cool, current, edgy, and timeless. The secret is her ability to expertly mix the tough and the tender, whether it's leather and lace or denim and diamonds. Nonchalance is her calling card. It's true; rock 'n' roll will never die, and this look will last forever.

IF THIS IS THE LOOK YOU'RE AFTER, ADD THESE PIECES TO YOUR BASICS:

- A FAUX FUR VEST
- A CROCHET PONCHO
- A DISTRESSED LEATHER JACKET
- A SEXY OVER-THE-KNEE BOOT (HEEL HEIGHT UP TO YOU)
- LARGE HOOP EARRINGS, STACKED RINGS AND BRACELETS
- A '70S-INSPIRED LEATHER PATCHWORK HOBO TOTE OR FRINGED HOBO BAG
- BLACK FRAMED, DARK TINTED SUNGLASSES

THE CLASSIC ROCK STAR: BIANCA JAGGER

WHO SHE IS: Nicaraguan-born Bianca Jagger is most famous for being the first wife of Rolling Stone Mick Jagger and one of the beautiful people who hung out at Studio 54, but she's also a well-respected political activist and campaigner for human rights who has worked with the British Red Cross and Amnesty International.

WHY SHE'S AN ICON: Even if the only photo of Bianca Jagger ever published was the one from her 1971 marriage to Mick in St. Tropez, for which she wore a white Yves Saint Laurent suit and a large veiled hat, she'd still be a fashion icon. This is one seriously stylish lady, known for her way with bowler hats, capes, oversized sunglasses, and her chic caftans.

"I DON'T WANT TO WEAR WHAT EVERY OTHER WOMAN WEARS.
I WON'T BE DICTATED TO."
—BIANCA JAGGER

THE BOMBSHELL

The Bombshell is completely feminine, ultra sexy, and always, always glamorous. This is the girl who will go the extra mile by wearing a matching bra-and-panty set—every day. Pencil skirts, halter necklines, and waist-cinching belts are wardrobe staples for her. Her jeans are perfectly fitted and her lips are always glossed. The Bombshell knows the value of her God-given curves and definitely how to enhance them. It's a look that might take some extra time and effort, but when the bombshell is running late, it's definitely worth the wait, and she always makes an entrance.

IF THIS IS THE LOOK YOU'RE AFTER, ADD THESE PIECES TO YOUR BASICS:

- A FORM-FITTING HALTER DRESS
- A CORSET-STYLE TOP
- MATCHING BRA-AND-UNDERWEAR SETS
- SATIN BLACK PLATFORM SANDALS
- A GLOSSY RED LIP AND FABULOUSLY FAKE LASHES
- CHANEL NO.5

THE CLASSIC BOMBSHELL: MARILYN MONROE

WHO SHE IS: Marilyn Monroe is, quite simply, the ultimate movie star. Born Norma Jeane Mortenson, she was one of the major box office draws of the 1950s and the era's biggest sex symbol.

WHY SHE'S AN ICON: Marilyn's blonde hair, breathy voice, and curvy figure set the gold standard for every starlet that followed. More importantly, in an era of twinsets and Peter Pan collars, the way she embraced her curves gave millions of women the confidence to dress in a way that emphasized and celebrated their sexuality, in body-conscious clothes and the all-important high heels. More than fifty years after her untimely death, Marilyn continues to charm and fascinate us.

"I'M VERY DEFINITELY A WOMAN AND I ENJOY IT."
—MARILYN MONROE

THE AVANT-GARDE

What the Avant-Gardist wears today, other ladies wear five years from now. Always ahead of the curve and often with an arty, intellectual twist to her style, this is one lady who's not afraid to take risks with her clothing choices. When every other woman in the room is wearing black, she's wearing red. When they're in dresses, she's in a menswear-inspired suit. The rule with her is: Expect the unexpected.

IF THIS IS THE LOOK YOU'RE AFTER, ADD THESE PIECES TO YOUR BASICS:

- AN ASYMMETRICAL TOP
- A MULTICOLOR, STATEMENT PRINT DRESS
- SKINNY BLACK PANTS
- GRAPHIC HEELS IN AN UNEXPECTED COLOR
- PIECES OF JEWELRY THAT EMULATE MODERN WORKS OF ART
- A UNIQUELY SHAPED HANDBAG OR CLUTCH WITH INTRICATE DETAILING AND HARDWARE

THE CLASSIC AVANT-GARDE: MARLENE DIETRICH

WHO SHE IS: Berlin-born Marie Magdalene "Marlene" Dietrich began her career as an actress in her native Germany before moving to Hollywood in 1930. A staunch anti-Nazi, she performed tirelessly for allied troops during World War II. In Hollywood this award-winning actress captivated audiences with her unique style and unrivaled talent.

WHY SHE'S AN ICON: It took a gutsy lady to wear a pants suit back in the 1930s, when one would never see women wearing slacks. It just didn't happen. But Marlene Dietrich, who made the menswear look her signature, was nothing if not ahead of her time, a true pioneer. Despite her penchant for pants, she still exuded the ultimate femininity. She's truly one of the most glamorous women of all time.

"I DRESS FOR MYSELF. NOT FOR THE IMAGE, NOT FOR THE PUBLIC, NOT FOR FASHION, NOT FOR MEN."

—MARLENE DIETRICH

DRESSING BY THE DECADE

TRUE: Fashion is all about self-expression. Also true: There are certain guidelines that just can't be ignored . . . and age is one of them. Like it or not, I believe your decade should dictate how you dress. Ignore this rule and you risk looking inappropriate and, if you push it far enough, ridiculous. It doesn't matter if you work out, wear sunscreen, drink gallons of water every day, and are constantly told you look young for your age. There are joys that come with every decade. Embrace them and you will look and feel your best. Being ageless today is about being timeless, not trendy.

"IN ORDER TO BE IRREPLACEABLE, ONE MUST ALWAYS BE DIFFERENT."
—COCO CHANEL

TWENTIES: THE TREND YEARS

If you're in your twenties, congratulations; when it comes to style, it's all about having a blast and trying it all on. Live it up and have major fun with fashion. This is the decade to experiment, explore, and create; play with trends; and try out everything. Be crazy. Be creative.

A word of caution from Uncle LZ: Don't give everything away! I see so many women in their twenties making mistakes like wearing things that are just too short, too tight, too revealing. They think "short and tight" means "sexy." On the contrary, I believe it just gives off the wrong impression. Trust me, it's far sexier and more appealing to have a bit of mystery . . .

THIRTIES: BUILDING YOUR FOUNDATION

Baby girl is growing up! By the time you reach your thirties, you probably have a pretty good idea of what you like and what your style is. You're more serious about your life and the choices you make. You're further along in your career and your wardrobe needs to reflect the woman you are becoming.

You should have a solid foundation of classic pieces that meet all your needs: a two-piece navy or black suit, tailored blouses, a little black dress, and a pencil skirt. You should now start investing in statement pieces, like a good handbag and a great, classic pair of designer shoes. Mix all of your new investment items with your existing wardrobe. One or two good classics can make an outfit look more expensive and important. And that translates into making you look more important . . . like I know you are! You can continue to experiment with trends in your thirties as you did in the previous decade, but be more selective. Embrace being a woman!

FORTIES: FIT AND FAB

If there's one thing I would say to women in their forties it would be this: Less fluff, more substance. In doing my makeovers, I've learned that this is an extremely interesting time for women—I've learned that there are those women who have a hard time letting go of how they dressed in their twenties and thirties and embracing a new decade when, in reality, a woman reaches her prime in her forties. The bottom line is that your forties are all about establishing your look, celebrating it, and owning it. Think of yourself as a fine bottle of wine; you keep getting better and better with age. #cheers

Choose colors that are classic and sophisticated like crème, black, navy, and gray, and you can never go wrong with jewel tones. Tailored pieces are key and work well with feminine details, such as a gorgeous tailored suit with a drape neck silk blouse. It's uber chic. When it comes to jewelry, invest in more solid, significant pieces, such as diamond studs and a luxury watch. Think substantial but understated; it's all in the detailing.

I firmly believe that women can look better as they age because they know themselves and they know what works. Don't fall into the trap of trying to dress like your teenage daughter—not only will your daughter be embarrassed by you (oh, Mom!), but you're not fooling anyone anyway.

FIFTIES: FABULOUS AND FIERCE

God bless Oprah Winfrey for saying that 50 is the new 30! There was a sigh of relief heard around the world when women suddenly realized that there's a lot more time left and that there was no reason to step out of the fashion spotlight. But use this time wisely!

This decade is all about defined, tasteful, interesting choices. Choosing your pieces wisely only gets more important as you age. Whenever I do a makeover I have the lucky woman stand in front of me in her bra and panties so I can see the specifics of what I'm working with and then decide what I need to do. And, yes, that initial conversation can be awkward at first, but ultimately it's a true bonding moment because they realize that I'm there to help them feel comfortable in their body and look amazing.

Women in their fifties tend to have the exact same response when they look in the mirror and see how gravity has taken control over their body and everything has made a beeline south. Life is in session and gravity takes its toll on all of us, but fortunately I know the clothes that will conceal troubled areas and create more confidence. More important than those key pieces that camouflage, I believe in the power of shapewear. That's right, never fear—your Fashion Guy is here! I said shapewear. You can either let everything keep falling, or stare gravity down and let shapewear lift you up.

SIXTIES: THE AGE OF ELEGANCE

There is nothing like seeing a well-dressed woman in her sixties. She knows exactly who she is, she dresses to please herself, and she doesn't give a damn what anyone else thinks. We should all aspire to live like this, but with age comes knowledge, and confidence.

In your sixties, elegance is essential. Choose hues in the same color family to give yourself a long, lean line. Pay attention to fit and choose your fabrics wisely.

As for trends, express yourself with accessories, especially scarves and jewelry. If you've given up on high heels, and I understand, I really do—try a sexy slingback with a kitten heel, or a chic wedge in the summer months and a wedged heel when it's colder. The main point is that just because you might have grandbabies, that doesn't mean you need to dress like a granny. I meet a lot of women in this age group who have a sort of Garanimals-style going on: loose, elastic waist pants; matching loose, floral blouse; and baggy, coordinating cardigan. I understand the effortlessness and comfort of buying these pieces, but pay attention to fit, tailoring, and accessorizing, which can transform those commonly used pieces to something chic and unique and most of all, still be comfortable.

SEVENTIES AND UP: DIGNIFIED AND DISTINGUISHED

You are an inspiration to all of us! Why not celebrate and, if your budget allows, indulge in some higher-end luxury items? It's a great way to honor the style you've spent decades perfecting.

At this age, women need to be more strategic about the fashion choices they make—your look should be dignified and distinguished. A well-cut suit will never fail you. But you can still live it up a bit. You've earned it, after all. Think exotic prints and bold colors or statement pieces that showcase your personality.

"I HAVE ALWAYS BELIEVED THAT FASHION WAS NOT ONLY TO MAKE WOMEN MORE BEAUTIFUL BUT ALSO TO REASSURE THEM, GIVE THEM CONFIDENCE."
—YVES SAINT LAURENT

LZ'S EXPERTS' GUIDE TO CREATING YOUR LOOK

One of the biggest thrills for me when making someone over is to help each woman find and create her own signature style. I have access to the best, most respected experts in town, whom I like to call my own personal "makeover dream team." Each one of these celebrated individuals not only works with the Hollywood elite, they have also become a cherished friend. #blessed

In the following pages, my "beauty VIPs" are spilling their invaluable style secrets, and helping guide you to create your own signature star style. Here you go—this info is like pure gold!

LOUIS LICARI'S TIPS FOR HAIR COLOR THAT MAKES YOU LOOK FIVE YEARS YOUNGER

LOUIS LICARI'S CALLING CARD

AKA THE "KING OF COLOR"

CELEBRITIES: SOFIA COPPOLA, JESSICA LANGE, SUSAN SARANDON

WEBSITE: WWW.LOUISLICARI.COM

TWITTER & INSTAGRAM: @LOUISLICARI

PINTEREST: LOUISLICARI

WHY COLOR? Color is the quickest way to brighten your look and add body and vibrancy to your hair. It can make a woman feel younger, fresher, and more vibrant, which makes her feel more confident. Depending on the placement of the color, you can actually make a woman's face appear thinner.

CHOOSE THE RIGHT COLOR. Hair color should always complement your complexion. That means that it should provide contrast to your skin color—if your hair and skin color are too similar, your hair color will wash out your face. The color you were born with gives you an idea of the color family that works for you, though it should be constantly evolving. Try a website that allows you to take a photo of your face and "try on" different colors and styles such as this one: www.instyle.com/instyle/makeover.

CONDITION RELIGIOUSLY. After coloring your hair, you really need to use a good deep-conditioning treatment. Louis Licari Instant Deep Treatment, which you can purchase on my website, works wonders on my clients. My entire line has the ionic color treatment that holds onto color longer. I also love L'Oreal EverPure Sulfate-Free Moisture Conditioner. Moroccan oil is fantastic for shine if your hair feels dry after coloring it.

TO COLOR OR NOT TO COLOR WHEN YOU'RE EXPECTING. I always recommend you consult with your OB-GYN before coloring your hair during pregnancy. If you do decide to color, I recommend sticking with highlights or lowlights (if your hair is gray) during pregnancy. This ensures that the hair color won't touch your scalp and is the safest way to color hair during your pregnancy.

LZ STYLE NOTE: Due to the fact that so many women are on the go with taking care of the kids, having a full-time job, and so on, getting to the hair salon for color and maintenance can be quite time-consuming. The miracle? At-home root touch-up systems or root concealers. You can either ask your professional colorist for their suggestions or go online and read beauty blogs for "how to" tips, product reviews, and recommendations.

OSCAR BLANDI'S TIPS ON GETTING AND MAINTAINING THE BEST HAIRCUT OF YOUR LIFE

OSCAR BLANDI'S CALLING CARD

CELEBRITIES: JULIANNE MOORE, JESSICA BIEL,

KELLY RIPA, ROSARIO DAWSON

WEBSITE: WWW.OSCARBLANDI.COM

TWITTER: @OSCARBLANDI

Here are Oscar's sexy Italian words of wisdom on choosing the perfect cut for the shape of your face:

ROUND: I prefer longer styles on rounder faces. You can add layers and side-swept bangs to add a little more edge.

HEART: A heart shape is similar to the triangle shape. Both long and short cuts work. If you decide to go short, make sure to leave a little length to frame the neckline—it is always sexy to have that natural line along your neck.

OBLONG: This face shape is most complemented by long, side-swept bangs or longer layers. (When hair is kept all one length on this shape, it can create the illusion that the hairline is receding.) You want to keep the front section (bangs or layers) long enough so that they can be swept off the face.

SQUARE: A square-shaped face can wear both short and long cuts well. What is most important to this face shape is dimension, whether by layering the cut to soften the angles or by sporting long bangs. Even a color contrast can create nice dimension and soften the face a bit.

BONUS:

READ LABELS. I designed my hair care products for every type of hair. (You can find my products at www.oscarblandi.com.) I also have good experiences with L'Oreal products. The brand has a lot of intelligence behind it in terms of research and development. When choosing a product, the less sulphates, alcohol, and ammonia, the better.

WASH YOUR HAIR. I always say people should treat their hair like they treat their skin. I don't suggest anyone wash their hair daily, to prevent it from drying out, and I am a huge fan of dry shampoo to keep it looking fresh before washes. Heat protectant products (serums, oils, sprays) are important because they seal the cuticle, meaning fewer split ends.

GLORIA WITHERSPOON-FRISKCO'S TIPS FOR GORGEOUS, STRESS-FREE AFRICAN-AMERICAN HAIR

GLORIA WITHERSPOON-FRISKCO'S CALLING CARD

CELEBRITIES: SHAKIRA, JESSICA ALBA, JULIANNA MARGULIES

WEBSITE: WWW.OSCARBLANDI.COM/STAFF_DETAIL.PHP?ID=33

TWITTER: @GFRISKCO

WASH AND WEAR. Believe it or not, African-American women really only need to wash their hair once or twice a week. Hair extensions should be washed once a week and should not be left in for longer than eight to ten weeks. Any longer, and you risk thinning the hair out and causing a lot of breakage.

PRACTICE SAFE STYLING. When it comes to styling, it's definitely a bad idea to use a flat iron, curling iron, or blow-dryer every day because the heat will dry out the hair and make it brittle. The only type of hair that can handle heat every day is hair extensions. When relaxing and coloring hair, it has to be two weeks apart or the hair will break off or fall out.

PRODUCTS THAT DON'T BREAK THE BANK. Silicon Mix makes a great shampoo and deep conditioner. I also like Giovanni Tea Tree Triple Treat Shampoo, Infusium 23 Shampoo and Infusium 23 Leave-In Treatment, and Garnier Fructis products.

DIANE D'AGOSTINO'S ULTIMATE NEW YORK PONYTAIL

DIANE D'AGOSTINO'S CALLING CARD

THREE-TIME EMMY®-WINNING HAIR STYLIST FROM

"LIVE WITH KELLY AND MICHAEL"

WEBSITE: WWW.STARSTYLEBEAUTY.COM

TWITTER: @DIANEDAGOSTINO

If you're always on the go, and you want to take your look from day to night, there's nothing more elegant or chic than the perfect New York ponytail. Take it away, Diane!

THE PERFECT NEW YORK PONYTAIL

STEP 1: Spray a thickening spray for extra body on dry hair.

STEP 2: Use a curling iron on 1" to 2" sections of hair to create waves all around your head. Loosen curls with your fingers.

STEP 3: Backcomb your hair at the crown with a wide-tooth comb.

STEP 4: Brush your hair back into a ponytail. You can make it at the nape of the neck or on the side, but the key to this look is that it needs to be low, not high. I like to match the color of the elastic band to the hair color for a refined look.

STEP 5: Complete the look with a finishing spray and, for evening, decorative accessories like a rhinestone clip.

BONUS TIPS FROM DIANE:

HAIR DRYER: I always tell my clients to invest in a really good blow-dryer because it dries the hair faster, and thereby minimizes frizz.

MASON PEARSON BRUSH: Another good investment is a Mason Pearson brush. Yes, it's expensive but the natural, boar bristles distribute the natural oils through your hair, leaving it silky and healthy looking.

HEALTHY, SEXY HAIR: There's a soy-paste product called Healthy Sexy Hair made by Sexy Hair that I absolutely love. It defines hair and leaves your hairstyle looking as if you just walked out of the salon.

FAUX IS FAB!

NOT ALL WOMEN ARE BORN WITH THICK, GLORIOUS HAIR. MORE OFTEN THAN NOT, WHAT YOU SEE IN MOVIES, TELEVISION, AND PRINT IS FABULOUS, FAKE HAIR. HAIR EXTENSIONS ARE HOTTER THAN EVER AND WHETHER YOU GO TO A SALON TO HAVE THEM DONE OR CLIP THEM IN YOURSELF, IT'S AN INSTANT SHOT OF SEXY CONFIDENCE. YOU CAN ADD BEAUTIFUL BANGS OR LAYER IN THICK, LONG LOCKS—IT'S YOUR CHOICE. IF YOU CAN'T AFFORD TO HAVE IT DONE PROFESSIONALLY (AND IT CAN BE PRETTY PRICEY, WITH TOP SALONS STARTING AT $500 FOR HAIR EXTENSIONS), CHECK OUT THESE TWO WEBSITES FOR ENDLESS OPTIONS AND STYLES FOR ALL TYPES OF HAIR—AND GET READY TO "CLIP IN" SOME GLAM!

WWW.HAIREXTENSIONS.COM

WWW.EXTENSIONS-PLUS.COM

MICHELLE CHAMPAGNE'S TIPS FOR PUTTING YOUR BEST FACE FORWARD

MICHELLE CHAMPAGNE'S CALLING CARD

TWO-TIME EMMY®-WINNING HAIR STYLIST FROM

"LIVE WITH KELLY AND MICHAEL"

WEBSITE: WWW.MICHELLECHAMPAGNE.COM

TWITTER: @MICHCHAMPAGNE

You might have a tendency to spend more time on your makeup when you're going out at night, but your daytime face is crying out for some love too! Here are Michelle's simple steps to a great, natural-looking daytime face. Michelle, you're up!

1. BUILD YOUR FOUNDATION: After you cleanse and moisturize, start with sheer foundation. Finding the right foundation will take some time. Your best solution is to consult a professional, whom you can find at your local department store makeup counters. I like to apply with fingertips, and then blend out with a sponge. Spot conceal and color correct with a camouflaging concealer and small concealer brush. Concentrate on the inner corner of eyes and around the nose, where skin tends to be a bit red or discolored.

LZ TIP Yellow-toned concealer is great at covering red spots, and pinky salmon-toned concealer is the perfect cover-up for that blue hue under the eyes.

2. POWDER POWER: The next step is to sweep a bit of loose translucent powder along the shine zone—your forehead, nose, the apples of your cheeks, and chin.

3. MAKE YOURSELF BLUSH: For a fresh glow, apply a pinky coral blush to the apples of cheeks in a circular sweeping motion that extends out to the hairline.

4. BRIGHTEN YOUR EYES: Frame the eyes with a strong, well-groomed brow. Fill in any sparse areas with a good eyebrow pencil, then brush with a little eyebrow gel. After that, apply a curling mascara to the root of the lashes and then wriggle your way up to the ends of the lashes. This will assure proper product placement and give you a more voluminous eyelash line. For added nighttime drama you can build a sultry smoky eye by smudging a kohl brown/black eyeliner across the lash line and blending in with sponge tip applicator. My go-to staple color on the eye is a brown shimmer. I sweep it onto the lids and blend a little under the bottom lash line and instantly create a sexy smoky eye.

5. PERFECT POUT: The finishing touch is the kisser. Always have a tinted lip balm in your bag. It is perfect for daytime wear and you can always build on that with some gloss for nighttime glamour.

5. BEAUTIFUL BROWS:

- TWEEZING, WAXING, AND THREADING ARE THREE WAYS TO ACHIEVE A WELL-GROOMED BROW.

- SHOP AROUND AND ASK FRIENDS WHEN SEARCHING FOR A QUALIFIED WAXER OR THREADER.

- DO NOT OVER-TWEEZE. SKINNY EYEBROWS CAN BE WAY TOO HARSH.

- THE ARCH OF THE BROW SHOULD PEAK AT THE OUTSIDE OF THE IRIS (NOT PUPIL).

- IF YOU HAVE BLONDE HAIR, YOUR BROWS SHOULD BE ONE SHADE DARKER, AND IF YOU HAVE DARK HAIR, THEY SHOULD BE ONE SHADE LIGHTER.

- SOME OF MY FAVORITE PRODUCTS TO HELP ACHIEVE A CLASSIC THICK BROW IS THE BROW PEN, FIBER FILLERS, AND TINTED BROW GEL.

- THE BROW PEN WORKS WELL ON VERY THIN BROWS TO HELP CREATE FAKE HAIRS BY WISPING IT IN THE SPARSE AREAS.

- FIBER FILLER USUALLY COMES IN A PEN AND HAS TINY HAIR-LIKE FIBERS THAT CAN GIVE VOLUME TO THE BROW.

- THE TINTED GEL CAN WRAP IT ALL UP BY FINISHING THE LOOK AND KEEPING THE HAIRS IN PLACE.

SONIA KASHUK'S DON'T-BREAK-THE-BANK MAKEUP BY THE DECADE

SONIA KASHUK'S CALLING CARD

WEBSITE: WWW.SONIAKASHUK.COM

FACEBOOK: WWW.FACEBOOK.COM/SONIAKASHUK

TWITTER & INSTAGRAM: @SONIAKASHUK

PINTEREST: SONIAKASHUKINC

There was a time when you had to go to high-end boutiques and department stores to find quality makeup products, and most women simply couldn't afford it. That was then—this is now. Keenly aware of this gap in the marketplace, Sonia successfully bridged it by creating her own, affordable makeup collection, sold exclusively at Target, because she believed beautiful, high-quality makeup doesn't have to cost a fortune.

As you've just read, I believe you should dress for your decade. When it comes to makeup, Sonia believes that specific rules apply too. Sonia, you're on!

SONIA'S MAKEUP TIPS FOR LOOKING DELICIOUS AT EVERY DECADE

20s Have fun. Experiment. Be colorful and playful! You can get away with nothing or something. Focus on the eyes, cheeks, and lips.

30s Start refining. Your makeup should be classic with a twist. You're growing up, but you also want a sense of surprise with rich colors. For example, an everyday smoky eye could work; use gray, taupe, and brown shades instead of black. This is perfect for day to night. For a twist, brighten up your pretty pout with a bright lip, such as fuchsia or coral.

40s Less is more. Go for softer, and lean toward nude color palettes. Too much makeup will always make you look older. Create a sweet balance of being pulled together.

50s Ladies, restart your engines. Start using more makeup, like concealer! Try a hint of color with your best bronzer and dial it up just a little more. Focus on neutral palettes. Utilize makeup trends to fix flaws; for example, lift the eyes by drawing out the liner with just a little in-and-upward stroke. Use makeup more precisely to counteract the aging process—to correct and enhance.

60s + UP Now, the motor's running. Continue using the same tips as the fifties but now add brightness to the cheek. Start using brightening primers that make the skin glow. You want a dewy, fresh, illuminated face that radiates and looks alive. Find products that bump up the skin and make you look young again. Have fun! Eyelashes can make a big difference. It's all about the nuances.

BEAU NELSON'S RED-CARPET GLAM

BEAU NELSON'S CALLING CARD

CELEBRITIES: KRISTEN STEWART, NICOLE RICHIE, JESSICA ALBA

WEBSITE: WWW.BEAUTE-COSMETICS.COM

TWITTER & INSTAGRAM: @BEAU_NELSON

When you're watching your favourite stars hit the red carpet at all the major award shows, you can rest assured that Beau Nelson is responsible for some of those fab faces.

BEAU'S PERFECT SMOKY EYE

To pull off a sultry smoky eye, use a long-wearing cream shadow instead of powder. Cream shadow blends more easily and you can move it around before it sets. Try this look with two cream shadows in the same color family, one darker for the nearest lash line and one lighter to help diffuse the color.

- First, apply the shadow with a small shadow brush to the eyelid, concentrating it at the lash line.

- Next, use a blending brush to diffuse it upward toward the crease and slightly above. It should look densest at the lashes and fade to nothing just below the brow bone.

- Then, use a small brush to sweep the shadow color around the bottom lash line, starting thicker on the outer edge and getting closer to the lashes the further you go toward the tear duct.

- For extra drama: add black pencil to the inner rim of the eye.

- Always finish with a lash curler and two coats of the blackest mascara you can find.

RED (LIP) ALERT

Red lipstick is a classic; it screams glamour and sophistication, and the right red makes a woman feel powerful and sexy. The best way to choose a red lipstick is to try a bunch on and see how each one makes you feel. In my experience, pale-skinned girls look great in blue-reds, medium-toned women look great in neutral and brick tones, and darker-skinned ladies look great in burgundy and orange-reds. Here's my perfect red-lip how-to:

1. Use a sharp lip pencil to define the lip edge and then fill in the entire lip with the pencil.

2. Then, take a clean, dry lip brush and blend the pencil into the lip and soften the edges of the lip line ever so slightly.

3. Apply a matching lipstick with the same brush over the pencil. This ensures a long-lasting lip color.

SOME OF BEAU'S MAKEUP MUST-HAVES:

- L'OREAL VOLUMINOUS CARBON BLACK MASCARA AND COVER GIRL CLUMP CRUSHER MASCARA
- MAYBELLINE CREAM EYESHADOW POTS
- MAC COSMETICS EYESHADOW
- NARS BRONZER
- CHANEL CRÉME BLUSH

DR. FREDRIC BRANDT'S TIPS FOR SKIN THAT LOOKS YOUNG ENOUGH TO GET YOU CARDED

DR. FREDRIC BRANDT'S CALLING CARD

CELEBRITIES: MADONNA (#VOGUE)

WEBSITE: WWW.DRFREDRICBRANDT.COM

TWITTER: @DRFREDRICBRANDT

DR. BRANDT'S THREE BASIC SKINCARE RULES:

1. Evening Routine: In the evening, cleanse your face thoroughly with a pH-balanced cleanser to keep your skin acidic, then apply a repairing collagen and elastin cream, such as a retinol or peptide cream.

2. Morning Routine: In the morning, use a sunscreen with an SPF of at least 30, as well as an antioxidant serum or cream that contains vitamin C, green tea, grape seed, white tea, soy, et cetera.

3. Once a Week: Exfoliate once a week with an at-home microdermabrasion cream or an at-home peel.

BOTOX ALTERNATIVES: There are several at-home products that will even out coloration and smooth fine lines and wrinkles. You can get prescription Retin-A or an over-the-counter retinol cream. There are also serums that contain ingredients that protect DNA and increase cellular respiration, like my new DNA Transforming Pearl Serum, which makes a tremendous difference in lines and wrinkles while firming skin.

BIG RESULTS, SMALL INVESTMENT: There are many good drugstore products, from Neutrogena to Oil of Olay. They offer a wide range of sunscreens (Neutrogena's Sensitive Skin Sunscreen Lotion SPF 60) and retinol serums (Olay's Regenerist Intensive Repair Treatment) to help improve skin. Lighten up: For age spots, there are many different over-the-counter remedies, but look for bleaching creams with ingredients such as liquorice extract or soy extract. For dark circles under eyes, look for products, such as ones with retinol, that will help up-regulate collagen production and decrease vascular congestion under the eye.

LZ TIP If you want Dr. Brandt to make a "house call," go to his website or www.sephora.com and find the right products for your skin type.

DEBORAH LIPPMANN'S TIPS ON NAILING A FLAWLESS MANI-PEDI

DEBORAH LIPPMANN'S CALLING CARD

CELEBRITIES: KATE WINSLET, REESE WITHERSPOON, RENEE ZELLWEGER, PENELOPE CRUZ

WEBSITE: WWW.DEBORAHLIPPMANN.COM

FACEBOOK: WWW.FACEBOOK.COM/DEBORAHLIPPMANN

TWITTER & INSTAGRAM: @DEBORAHLIPPMANN

TUMBLR: HTTP://DEBORAHLIPPMANN.TUMBLR.COM

NAIL MAINTENANCE. Both short and long nails need a weekly manicure, either at home or at the salon. Make sure all the nails are the same length and shape and the cuticles are pushed back. Foot care is extremely important, too. Going to the salon to get a pedicure isn't enough—regular maintenance is key. Keep a foot scrub, foot file, and callus softener in the shower year-round—not just in the summer!—and spend 30 seconds on each foot at least twice a week to keep feet feeling and looking great. As for toenails, the length of the toenail should never hang over the toe. Be sure not to clip the sides of the nails at an angle or you risk ingrown nails. File straight across and just gently round the corners.

BE CAREFUL WHAT YOU CUT. Your cuticles are there to act as a barrier for bacteria, so I don't believe you should cut them. My Cuticle Remover is a convenient way to care for and maintain your cuticles each week. Hydrating is important, too. Our nails look a lot better when we're properly hydrated. Moisturize your hands with hand cream or cuticle oil every time you wash your hands.

EXFOLIATE. Just like your skin, your nails need to be exfoliated to be strong and healthy. Use a nail buffer like my Smooth Operator. It will make polish easier to apply and the buffing action helps blood nourish the matrix, which in turn helps the nail grow.

LZ TIP To purchase Deborah's colorful collection of products, check out her website.

CELEBRITY DENTIST BILL DORFMAN'S TIPS FOR A HIGH-WATTAGE HOLLYWOOD SMILE

BILL DORFMAN, DDS, CALLING CARD

CELEBRITIES: ANNE HATHAWAY, USHER,

EVA LONGORIA, JESSICA SIMPSON

TWITTER: @DRBILLDORFMAN

FACEBOOK: WWW.FACEBOOK.COM/DRBILLDORFMAN

WEBSITE: WWW.BILLDORFMANDDS.COM

YOUTUBE CHANNEL: WWW.YOUTUBE.COM/USER/DRBILLDORFMAN

WHITEN THE PROFESSIONAL WAY: When it comes to whitening your teeth, for the safest, fastest results, go to an accredited cosmetic dentist. This is an investment, but the results are instant and quite astounding. Beautiful, white teeth can dramatically freshen up your entire look and enhance your appearance. "Touch ups" can be administered every four to six months as needed.

OVER-THE-COUNTER WHITENERS: As for drugstore products, only use the ones that have been approved by the American Dental Association (ADA). If you have any questions or concerns, call your dentist for guidance.

YOUR DAILY SMILE: For daily care, brush and floss after every meal and scrape your tongue daily!

LZ TIP If you want any of Dr. Bill's dental care products, then style your way to his website and get ready to smile.

TOP FIVE TAKEAWAYS FROM LZ'S SIXTH COMMANDMENT

ONE   KNOW WHAT STYLES SUIT YOU AND YOUR BODY—JUST BECAUSE IT'S IN STYLE, IT MIGHT NOT BE THE STYLE FOR YOU.

TWO   PICK A STYLE ICON TO HELP YOU FOCUS AND FINESSE YOUR LOOK.

THREE   DRESS FOR YOUR ACTUAL DECADE (NOT THE AGE YOU WISH YOU WERE!).

FOUR   CHOOSE THE RIGHT HAIRCUT AND COLOR TO ACCENTUATE AND COMPLEMENT YOUR FACE SHAPE AND BEAUTIFUL FEATURES.

FIVE   WEAR MAKEUP APPROPRIATELY FOR YOUR DECADE WHILE YOU CREATE YOUR OWN STAR STYLE. #YOURNAMELIGHTS

7 | THOU SHALT SHOP WISELY (AND ONLINE!)

"IT'S NOT THE HAVING, IT'S THE GETTING."

—ELIZABETH TAYLOR

Now that you have an idea of the style you want to create—here's the fun part—let's go shopping! Yay! My seventh commandment for a perfect wardrobe is all about shopping like a stylist. How does a stylist shop? They always, always start with a goal and a plan! By utilizing specific insider secrets, I'm going to teach you how to make shopping stress-free and fun, whether it's online or in the store. It's all here; everything you need to know to become a highly trained and successful shopper.

If there's one thing I've learned from the countless makeovers I've done, it's that shopping is tough for women. All women are not created equal, and finding pieces to suit you, your size, and your shape can be challenging, frustrating, and exhausting. But I want to take the pain and misery out of shopping and show you how it can be fun, if you go about it the right way.

A PLAN: DON'T LEAVE HOME WITHOUT IT

Yes, shopping can be overwhelming and time-consuming. Don't worry, because I'm going to teach you "LZ's ultimate way to shop." The most important rule for shopping wisely: Even before you grab your keys and head for the door, you've got to do your research. No stylist heads for the sales floor without a solid game plan—they know exactly what they need to buy and where they're going to find it. To a stylist, shopping is a J-O-B and I want you to think of it that way, too. From now on, you won't just run over to the mall thinking you'll grab whatever catches your eye. You'll first (and quickly) create a plan and a goal.

For the sake of simplicity, let's say you need a new pair of black pants. Okay, that's your goal. But now you need a more specific plan—you need to do a little prep work and decide on the exact pair of pants you want. Are they dressy, for work, or casual? Get online and suss out different silhouettes,

BE A BUDGET BABE

BUDGET? WHAT'S THAT? HERE ARE MY TOP TIPS FOR CREATING A FASHION-CONSCIOUS BUDGET AND STICKING TO IT.

USE THE INTERNET. THERE ARE MANY MONEY PLANNING WEBSITES OUT THERE THAT WILL HELP YOU FIGURE OUT WHAT YOU HAVE COMING IN AND GOING OUT EVERY MONTH. A FEW I RECOMMEND ARE MINT.COM (WWW.MINT.COM), BUXFER (WWW.BUXFER.COM), AND MONEY STRANDS (HTTPS://MONEY.STRANDS.COM).

DIFFERENTIATE BETWEEN "NEED" AND "WANT." NOT ALWAYS EASY, I KNOW, BUT GETTING THIS STRAIGHT CAN SAVE YOU A BUNDLE. YES, WE ALL WANT THINGS, BUT SOMETIMES OUR BUDGET WON'T ALLOW IT. WHAT WE NEED ARE THE NECESSITIES.

DON'T IMPULSE SHOP. IF YOU SEE SOMETHING YOU LIKE, PUT IT DOWN, WALK AWAY, GRAB A COFFEE, DO SOME OTHER SHOPPING, AND THEN GO BACK TO THE COVETED ITEM. ASK YOURSELF HOW MANY DIFFERENT WAYS YOU CAN WEAR THAT ONE ITEM. OTHER THAN "SPECIAL OCCASION DRESSES," YOU SHOULD BE ABLE TO CREATE AT LEAST THREE OR FOUR DIFFERENT LOOKS WITH IT. ONCE YOU'VE ANSWERED THAT QUESTION, THEN YOU CAN MAKE THE PROPER DECISION. IF YOU FIND YOURSELF ON THE FENCE, THEN PASS. I GUARANTEE YOU WON'T EVEN REMEMBER IT IN THE MORNING.

FAMILIARIZE YOURSELF WITH OFF-PRICE RETAILERS (20-60 PERCENT OFF DEPARTMENT STORE PRICES), CONSIGNMENT SHOPS, AND OUTLETS. THERE ARE SO MANY SHOPPING OPTIONS THAT DON'T INVOLVE PAYING FULL PRICE. GET CREATIVE!

SHOP OFF-SEASON. BUYING YOUR WINTER COAT IN THE SPRING AND YOUR BATHING SUIT IN THE FALL CAN MEAN SIGNIFICANT SAVINGS AND GIVE YOU SOMETHING TO LOOK FORWARD TO.

BOOKMARK SOME SAVINGS. THERE ARE MANY WEBSITES OUT THERE DEDICATED TO HELPING FASHION LOVERS SAVE MONEY. I LOVE THE BUDGET FASHIONISTA (WWW.THEBUDGETFASHIONISTA.COM), FRUGAL FASHIONISTAS (HTTP://FRUGAL-FASHIONISTAS.COM), AND THE RECESSIONISTA (WWW.THERECESSIONISTA.COM).

materials, and prices. (A couple of sites to consider are www.net-a-porter.com and www.shopbop.com, as they have fantastic trend pages.) Or, just google "black pants" and see what pops up! You'll have pages and pages of ideas, designers, price points, and more.

> "I LIKE MY MONEY RIGHT WHERE I CAN SEE IT . . . HANGING IN MY CLOSET."
> —CARRIE BRADSHAW, *SEX AND THE CITY*

Once you have a good idea of the type of black pants you're targeting, carve out at least three to four hours to look for them. Yes, I said hours, not 15 minutes in between ten million other errands; this is something you can't rush. You may come to a point when you can cruise a store and nail what you need in no time, but for now, it's like you're in kindergarten and just learning to read . . . slowly and word for word. Also, consider bringing a friend whose fashion sense you admire; it's nice to have a second opinion when you shop.

DRESS FOR (SHOPPING) SUCCESS

Think of going shopping as similar to going into battle. You've got to be fully prepared, ready for anything. Instead of capturing a military target, your mission is to hunt down and find the perfect pair of black pants. Before heading out, eat a good breakfast. Pack a tote with a few essentials: a bottle of water, a power bar, some handy wipes, hand sanitizer, a handheld mirror, a phone charger, and a pair of pumps. Wear the right undergarments. (It is pointless to shop for slim-fitting black pants if you're wearing baggy underwear.) If you're shopping for a backless dress, don't wear a sports bra. If you're shopping for heels, don't wear sweats. I think you get the idea . . . and most importantly don't forget to take stock of what's in your closet so you don't buy duplicates of what you already have.

Now that you're suited up, prepped, and ready for your mission, pause for a moment, take a deep breath, and make an agreement with yourself to have some fun. This time, you have a clear objective, you've created the space in your day, you're going to stay on course, and you're going to be victorious.

WISE SHOPPING = CHOICES, CHOICES, CHOICES

I understand the appeal of shopping in cute little boutiques, but for your first foray into shopping like a stylist, I suggest you head to a large department store because that's where you're going to find the biggest selection of designers, styles, and price points to suit your budget. Just as good real estate is all about location, location, location, good shopping is all about choices, choices, choices. And for this initial trip, it's all about seeing as many options as you can. Once you walk into that store, the hunt for the perfect black pants is on! But don't make the mistake of being uber picky from the get-go. The idea is to try on many different pairs, so pick up every single pair of black pants that you gravitate toward. That's right; if it catches your eye even for a second, don't ignore that gut reaction. Also, don't make assumptions about size—grab a couple of sizes of each pair because even within a single brand, cuts can vary widely. Once you have a big stack (and I mean big!), head for the dressing room and start trying them on.

Look at yourself in the mirror, and examine your body from every angle and ask yourself the following questions:

THE WISE SHOPPER'S DRESSING ROOM Q&A:

- HOW DO THE PANTS HANG ON YOUR BODY?
- HOW DOES YOUR BUTT LOOK IN THEM?
- DO THEY NEED EXTENSIVE TAILORING?

- HOW DOES THE FABRIC FEEL AGAINST YOUR SKIN?
- DO THEY NEED TO BE DRY-CLEANED?
- WHAT CUT IS MOST FLATTERING ON YOUR BODY?
- DO YOU HAVE THE PROPER SHOES AT HOME THAT WILL WORK WITH THEM?
- DO THEY GO WITH OTHER THINGS IN YOUR CLOSET?
- HOW DO THEY FEEL WHEN YOU SIT DOWN, STAND UP, AND BEND OVER?

As you work your way through the pile, ask yourself the above questions and weed out the pants that don't give you the right answers. In the end, you'll have a couple of pairs left. One of those, or maybe even two, are your new black pants. Congratulations! You've just shopped like a pro. Tiring, perhaps, but you've just emerged victorious.

Whether you realize it or not, you've done more than find a pair of pants. You've learned about what you like and what styles flatter your body, and you've discovered how to think about what works with the items you've already got in your closet. That's a day well spent investing in your shopping expertise.

YOU CAN SHOP WITH THE PROS

Insider tip: If you want to shop with a stylist, you can. Now, as much as I would love to go shopping with you myself, I'm actually talking about the professional shopping services offered by many department stores.

That's right; Bloomingdale's, Neiman Marcus, Nordstrom, and Macy's all have free shopping services. I can tell you from my experience working with the team at Macy's By Appointment that this type of service is invaluable, free, and makes shopping such a pleasant experience. These trained individuals are not only up to speed on what's in style and in stock, they also treat their customers like Hollywood stars.

THE BARGAIN BASEMENT GOES HIGH-END

FOR MY DESIGNER DIVAS WHO CRAVE THE LABEL, DON'T THINK YOU HAVE TO PAY FULL PRICE TO GET THE BRANDS YOU'RE LUSTING AFTER. THESE OFF-PRICE RETAILERS OFFER DESIGNER NAMES FOR A FRACTION OF THE COST OF MAINSTREAM STORES. DON'T LIVE NEAR ONE? CHECK OUT THEIR WEBSITES.

- MARSHALLS (WWW.MARSHALLSONLINE.COM)
- T.J. MAXX (WWW.TJMAXX.COM)
- CENTURY 21 (WWW.C21STORES.COM)
- LOEHMANN'S (WWW.LOEHMANNS.COM)
- NORDSTROM RACK (WWW.NORDSTROMRACK.COM)

LET'S GET VIRTUAL: HOW TO SHOP ONLINE

I'm a big fan of shopping online. If the town you live in doesn't have a good department store or boutique, it's genius. If you love the idea of shopping in your pajamas after you've put the kids to bed and poured yourself a glass of wine, it's also genius. There's a reason so many online retailers see an increase in traffic at about 9 p.m. — it's because it's mommy time = shopping time. The best part about shopping online and having everything sent to you is that you don't fight the hassle of department stores and the ugly lighting in the dressing room. Instead, you get to try on everything in the comfort of your own home and see how these news pieces will or won't work with your existing wardrobe! And for those pieces that don't suit you and your wardrobe, you're not stuck with them; the return policies are generally super easy.

SIZING UP THE SITUATION

IF YOU'RE PETITE, TALL, OR PLUS-SIZE, SHOPPING CAN POSE EXTRA CHALLENGES. YOU CAN SOMETIMES GET BY WITH ALTERATIONS, BUT FOR THOSE TIMES WHEN YOU WANT TO SHOP YOUR SIZE, HERE ARE THE PLACES THAT HAVE YOU IN MIND, WHETHER SHOPPING IN-STORE OR ONLINE:

PETITE: THOUGH NOT SPECIFICALLY GEARED TOWARDS PETITES, THESE RETAILERS ALL OFFER A GOOD SELECTION OF CLOTHES IN SMALLER SIZES.

- BANANA REPUBLIC (WWW.BANANAREPUBLIC.COM)
- TALBOTS (WWW.TALBOTS.COM)
- ANNE KLEIN (WWW.ANNEKLEIN.COM)

TALL: FOR THOSE OF YOU LOOKING FOR LONGER INSEAMS AND BLOUSES THAT COVER YOUR TORSO, THESE SITES ARE GENIUS:

- TALL COUTURE (WWW.TALLCOUTURE.COM)
- LONG ELEGANT LEGS (WWW.TALLWOMENSCLOTHES.COM)
- SIMPLY TALL (WWW.SIMPLYTALL.NET)

PLUS-SIZE: AS FOR FULL-FIGURED FASHION, TRY THESE RETAILERS ON FOR SIZE:

- LANE BRYANT (WWW.LANEBRYANT.COM)
- ASOS CURVE (WWW.ASOS.COM)
- ZARA (WWW.ZARA.COM)
- CATHERINES (WWW.CATHERINES.COM)
- FOREVER 21 (WWW.FOREVER21.COM)
- NORDSTROM (WWW.NORDSTROM.COM)

MAXIMIZE YOUR ONLINE SHOPPING EXPERIENCE

With online shopping, there's a right and a wrong way to go, and you know I'm not going to let you go wrong. First, make sure you read all of the information for each website. Every company has its own way of doing things and you need to make sure you understand the rules and return policies.

HERE'S SOME OF WHAT YOU SHOULD LOOK FOR BEFORE YOU CLICK "ADD TO SHOPPING CART":

MEASUREMENTS: The best online retailers measure their clothes for you. This is much more helpful than having just the size info because, as we all know, sizes can vary, even within a brand.

FIT TIPS: If an online retailer suggests you order up or down a size, then you should order up or down a size. Online fit tips are general guidelines to give you an idea of what to expect. To be safe, you should always order multiple sizes. You keep what fits and send back everything else.

FABRIC CONTENT AND CARE INSTRUCTIONS: You read this in the store, don't you? (Don't you?) Do the same online. If you know you're never going to hand wash a silk blouse, don't order it. See? I just made your life easier. You're welcome!

REVIEWS: This the most ingenious aspect of shopping online. You've basically got the world supporting you when you shop. The reviews let you know what another woman thought of the very item of clothing you're thinking of buying—what she liked, what she didn't like, why she ended up returning it.

THE RETURN POLICY: Online return policies are typically very fair. You'll get a good block of time to try something on and send it back if it doesn't work. Often retailers will pay for shipping both ways. But read these policies carefully, because they vary from site to site and they can change for sale items.

SHOP 'TIL YOU DROP: LZ'S FAVE ONLINE RETAILERS

From special occasion dresses to clothes for your husband and kids and everything in between, here are some online retailers that are definitely worth checking out. These are my personal go-tos, and I think many of them will become yours too!

ADORN (WWW.ADORN.COM): If you want special occasion jewelry, Adorn lets you rent the real deal, much of it inspired by red-carpet and celebrity designs. Want to try Kate Middleton's earrings for the night? They're here.

ASOS (WWW.ASOS.COM): This British site is an acronym for As Seen On Screen, ships to more than 190 countries, and lets you pay a yearly fee for unlimited overnight delivery. It's got everything from beauty to fashion, and it's all on-trend.

BAG BORROW OR STEAL (WWW.BAGBORROWORSTEAL.COM): When you want the bag but don't have the funds, why not rent it? Bag Borrow or Steal lets you take (temporary) ownership of some of the hottest designer styles of the season.

CLASSIC SHAPEWEAR (WWW.CLASSICSHAPEWEAR.COM): From bras to panties and everything in between, this is your one-stop shop for everything shapewear-related. All the big brands are here, including Spanx, Bali, Le Mystere, and Skinnygirl. Get your sexy on . . . online!

CLUB MONACO (WWW.CLUBMONACO.COM): No one does classic interpretations of the trends like Club Monaco, from classic silk blouses to terrific tanks, and an assortment of chic dresses. Their designer collaborations are worth looking at, too, and don't forget to check out the accessories.

DAVID'S BRIDAL (WWW.DAVIDSBRIDAL.COM): Bridal gowns, tuxedos, prom dresses—David's makes special occasion shopping easy, stylish, and most of all, affordable. When it comes to choosing a wedding dress based on your shape and size, they have a guide that will help you make the right choice and ensure that you'll look beautiful on your special day.

FARFETCH (WWW.FARFETCH.COM): This website unites high-end boutiques from all over the world that will ship right to your door for a reasonable fee—no import duties or unexpected charges to deal with. It's like shopping in Paris or Milan without leaving your sofa. Ooh la la.

GILT GROUP (WWW.GILT.COM): This members-only site is the ultimate online sample sale, with fresh designer goods going on sale daily. Sign up (it's free) and join the movement. (FYI: Gilt is not just about how you look, it's about how you live. They have everything from home décor, travel, and many other things your stylish heart desires at a discounted price.)

H&M (WWW.HM.COM): Every trend, every color, every season, plus an amazing selection of kid's clothes. When it comes to buying what's in style at a SUPER affordable price, the Swedes know what they're doing.

JCPENNEY (WWW.JCPENNEY.COM): Everything you love about JCP with the convenience of online. A gazillion labels, plenty of choices, and reasonable prices. How can you go wrong?

J.CREW (WWW.JCREW.COM): Thanks to the brilliant vision of creative director Jenna Lyons, J.Crew has gone from preppy outfitter to fashion-insider obsession. Great for coats, sweaters, chinos, and the all-important pencil skirt. Plus I'm obsessed with their jewelry; from statement necklaces to cool cocktail rings, they have the jewelry to dress you up! And, their sales are AH-MAY-ZING!

LANDS' END (WWW.LANDSEND.COM): Swimsuits to parkas, done. They carry sizes for everyone! Don't forget to check out the tote bags, towels, flip-flops, and everything else you need for the beach.

MACY'S (WWW.MACYS.COM): When it comes to places I love to shop, Macy's is definitely at the top of the list. The selection is second to none, and there's something for every budget.

MAURICES (WWW.MAURICES.COM): When you're in need of an accessory update or a super-affordable fashion fix, look no further than Maurices. Their $8 cocktail rings will definitely knock your eyes out.

MOD CLOTH (WWW.MODCLOTH.COM): Founded by high school sweethearts—awww!—this site takes a democratic approach to fashion with its "Be the Buyer" program that lets you vote styles from emerging designers onto the site. Great for retro-style dresses and tops.

NASTY GAL (WWW.NASTYGAL.COM): Don't judge a website by its title, ladies. For my younger girls who are anything but nasty, this site has on-trend, price-is-right fashion that's fun, spirited, and easy to wear.

NET-A-PORTER (WWW.NET-A-PORTER.COM): The stylish grandmother of all fashion retailers, Net-a-Porter still carries one of the best designer selections on the web and offers unparalled customer service—definitely try their stylist service. When you're looking to splurge, look no further.

OLD NAVY (WWW.OLDNAVY.COM): Old Navy has some of the best prices in town for basics such as jeans, cardigans, chinos, and T's, plus their kids clothes are crazy cool. I also love them for men's staples like polo shirts and cargo shorts.

THE OUTNET (WWW.THEOUTNET.COM): Net-a-Porter's sister site is devoted to deeply discounted designer fashion from more than 200 brands and counting. And just like its more upscale sibling, it's a pleasure to shop. This one's addictive, ladies.

PIPERLIME (WWW.PIPERLIME.COM): Part of the Gap/Old Navy/Banana Republic family, this site focuses on selling shoes, clothing, and accessories from a variety of labels. There is plenty to find for under $75 and the free shipping/free returns/no minimum policy makes life super easy.

RENT THE RUNWAY (WWW.RENTTHERUNWAY.COM): The Netflix of fashion, with a genius concept: instead of paying top dollar for delicious designer duds, you can rent them. And the execution is brilliant, with customer reviews, many of which feature photos that let you judge the way a dress will look on a real body before you click "buy."

SHOPBOP (WWW.SHOPBOP.COM): This cult-following site started as a brick-and-mortar store in Wisconsin and now draws shoppers from all over the world. They keep coming back for the well-edited selection of trends and classic pieces, including plenty of designer exclusives. Check out its brother site for men, East Dane (www.eastdane.com).

SOLE SOCIETY (WWW.SOLESOCIETY.COM): A MUST for shoes. Their styles range from classics to right-off-the-runway inspirations, at prices that will not break the bank and give you "sole." (Another fashion funny!)

SPORT CHALET (WWW.SPORTCHALET.COM): One of the web's best destinations that will help you look great while you get your sport on, with a huge selection of name brands in stock.

TARGET (WWW.TARGET.COM): Their own stuff is cute but let's be honest, the reason to shop at Target is for the designer collaborations, which are second to none. Move fast, though; they sell out in the blink of an eye.

UNDER ARMOUR (WWW.UNDERARMOUR.COM): Another great workout wear retailer. If you're not sure how much support you need from a sport bra, their guide will help you figure it out.

YOOX (WWW.YOOX.COM): If you like high-end, don't say yes, say Yoox. This site offers designer fashions at steep discounts.

7APPOS (WWW.ZAPPOS.COM): A fantastic selection of shoes for the entire family and one of the best return policies on the web: You get 365 days to decide whether those pumps are made for walking or not.

ZARA (WWW.ZARA.COM): As you know, all great things start with Z. Like Zarian, Zara is a style destination, too. If there's not one in your town for an in-person visit, log on to Zara immediately. New stock arrives constantly and all of it, from shoes to blouses to coats, is up to date and just so chic.

LZ'S BUYING GUIDE

Here are some of my top tips for when you need to purchase specific items. And these tips apply whether you're shopping in-person or online.

A WINTER COAT: Go up a size. You're going to be layering a sweater under it and you don't want to look like the Michelin man. Your coat will not look too big because you can always get it tailored.

A CASHMERE SWEATER: This is one item where you get what you pay for, so my advice is to save up and buy classic. The best cashmere is made from extra-long fibers. Cheap cashmere is made from short fibers that will pill. When you've made the splurge, treat it with care. Stick with classic colors like black, charcoal gray, chocolate brown, and rich cream.

WORK SHOES: When buying shoes online, get an assortment of sizes and stick with the designers that you've worn before. With shoes, it's all about the fit and knowing what works for you.

A BATHING SUIT: When it comes to buying bathing suits at a department store or boutique, this can be extremely difficult and quite uncomfortable. In order to ease the pain, and have some privacy, I suggest that you shop for swimwear online and invest in quality-made suits. One of my absolute favorite places for women to shop for swimwear is Lands' End. They carry a vast assortment of sizes, styles, and shapes for every woman. Their designers have truly designed flattering swimwear that women can wear with confidence. From their elaborate "swimsuit" glossary and "fit and sizing" chart, to swimwear with sun protection, they have made swimsuit shopping easy, fun, and fast. Most importantly, always order an assortment of styles and sizes and see what feels and fits best at home. Lands' End also carries a wonderful assortment of the all-important cover-up, too.

A SPECIAL OCCASION DRESS: Hollywood has the Oscars®, you have your own "real life" red carpet and you want to look your best for it. You can find beautiful dresses at most department stores and online retailers. But two of my favorite places to send women for dresses are Macy's and Bloomingdale's. They have such an eclectic collection of styles of special occasion dressing for all shapes, styles, and price points. Since this is a special occasion, buy your dress well in advance and give it a trial run at least a week before you plan on wearing it. Consider this a full dress rehearsal, with everything from shapewear to makeup to heels on. Make sure you're comfortable. Sit. Stand. Walk around your house in your heels. Does anything pinch? Does anything feel awkward? Shift? Fall out? Give yourself a week and you've got time to fix any problems that crop up.

"A WOMAN'S DRESS SHOULD BE LIKE A BARBED-WIRE FENCE: SERVING ITS PURPOSE WITHOUT OBSTRUCTING THE VIEW."
—SOPHIA LOREN

A SUIT: Go for a classic, well-tailored cut instead of something trendy. This means you should avoid epaulettes, intricate trims, elaborate buttons, and anything else that screams, "This will be out of style next year." These things will come and go like the tide but basic and black equals forever. And don't think you always have to wear the suit as an outfit. Separate those pieces, move them throughout your wardrobe, and let the mixing and matching begin.

CALLING ALL SAVVY SHOPPERS: IT'S SHOWTIME!

You're invited to LZ's Shopping Extravaganza Fashion Show

PLACE: Your House
TIME: Any time you like
DRESS: Fabulous
RSVP: Consider it done

If you've been following my commandments religiously (pun intended), you now have a good understanding of which styles and designers suit you and what you need to have in your wardrobe to create your personal style.

Now it's time to invite a few of your favorite girlfriends over and host your own at-home fashion show in order to show off your new pieces you found in-store or online. Here's how it works: You pick a date several weeks in advance and email your invitation. Go easy on yourself and make it a potluck. You supply the wine; everyone else brings nibbles. Ask everyone to bring the new outfits and pieces they've purchased recently.

Push back the chairs and the tables and make a runway in your living room. If you really want to go big, you can even get a roll of red carpet from a carpet discounter (check online for one in your area). I've done this for TV makeovers and it always goes over well—there's something about walking on a red carpet that gets everyone posing like they're walking down the red carpet at the Academy Awards®. Set up a buffet table for snacks and drinks. Get some flowers and light a scented candle. The idea is to make the atmosphere as glamorous as possible!

LIGHTS, CAMERA, ACTION

Ask the girls to arrive camera-ready: hair and makeup done and shapewear on. Once everyone's there and has had a glass of wine or something bubbly, you're ready to start. Everyone gets dressed in her first outfit and then take turns strutting your stuff on the "runway." Crank the music up and let the fashion show begin!

Once everyone has done her thing, go from girl to girl and talk about what worked and why. Remember, this is a love fest—you're not breaking anybody down. Then you go back around again and talk about things that could be improved—Does it need a statement necklace? A scarf? A higher pair of heels? Or, share with your friends what worked and why. As friends, the words you say will be laced with kindness and love, and this fashion show is to help, so whatever you say should be framed as creative and kind commentary. Sometimes getting a little advice from your most honest and stylish friends goes a long way while you're creating your new style.

"IT'S A NEW ERA IN FASHION—THERE ARE NO RULES. IT'S ALL ABOUT THE INDIVIDUAL AND PERSONAL STYLE, WEARING HIGH-END, LOW-END, CLASSIC LABELS, AND UP-AND-COMING DESIGNERS ALL TOGETHER."
—ALEXANDER MCQUEEN

Most importantly, and I do this with every makeover, you should take out your camera or phone and take photos of every outfit from every angle, so you can see what you like from the front, back, and sides. When taking a photo, you can also see what catches your eye, and what needs to be added or taken off. You can even make a video of the whole evening. Seeing things in movement makes a huge difference, kids. You notice details that you just don't see in a photo. Once the night is over, you'll have a clear understanding of the pieces you're keeping and the ones you're returning. Not only is it lots of fun, but it'll bring you closer to your friends in a unique way. Take turns hosting those fun, fashionable nights and try to do them once a season.

ACCESSORY SWAP

HERE'S A FUN IDEA TO IMPROVE YOUR ACCESSORY WARDROBE WHEN YOU'RE BUDGET-CONSCIOUS. RATHER THAN GOING OUT AND BUYING ACCESSORIES LIKE FUN COSTUME JEWELRY, BELTS, HATS, AND SCARVES, JUST HAVE YOUR GIRLFRIENDS (THE ONES THAT SHOW UP FOR THE FASHION SHOW) BRING A BAG OF THEIR OWN ACCESSORIES AND THEN DURING THE EVENING, YOU SWAP BAGS. YOU KEEP SOMEONE ELSE'S BAG FOR THE SEASON AND GET TO TRY THEIR ACCESSORIES ON YOUR WARDROBE.

SWEETHEART, I GUARANTEE YOU, IF YOU SHOW UP AT WORK OR DINNER WITH NEW AND EXCITING ACCESSORIES, YOU'LL GET COM-PLIMENTS, AND YOU GET TO SEE YOUR CLOTHES IN A WHOLE NEW LIGHT. AT THE END OF THE SEASON, YOU GIVE YOUR BAG BACK TO ITS OWNER. THOUGH DON'T BE SURPRISED IF YOU END UP DOING SOME PERMANENT SWAPPING. #LOVETHAT

TOP FIVE TAKEAWAYS FROM LZ'S SEVENTH COMMANDMENT

ONE NEVER GO SHOPPING WITHOUT A GAME PLAN KNOW WHAT YOU WANT TO BUY, WHERE YOU'RE GOING TO SHOP, AND HOW MUCH YOU CAN SPEND.

TWO DON'T PAY FULL PRICE FOR THE DESIGNER LABELS THAT YOU LOVE. SHOP OFF-PRICE RETAILERS.

THREE ALWAYS TRY ON MULTIPLE SIZES FROM A VARIETY OF DESIGNERS.

FOUR SHOP ONLINE AND THEN TRY ON EVERYTHING IN THE LUXURY OF YOUR OWN HOME.

FIVE INVITE YOUR BESTIES OVER AND HOST AN AT-HOME FASHION SHOW. #SUPERMODELS

8 | THOU SHALT DRESS YOUR MAN

"MENSWEAR IS ABOUT SUBTLETY.
IT'S ABOUT GOOD STYLE AND GOOD TASTE."

—ALEXANDER MCQUEEN

By now, you're building quite a bit of confidence in your wardrobe and you know exactly how to make your own style statements. But if you're dressed to the nines and feeling fab, there's nothing worse than being embarrassed by the appearance of the guy by your side. If your man is in need of his own style overhaul, but you think it's a hopeless cause, think again. I'm going to show you how to turn his wardrobe around and help him look his absolute best. Trust me, ladies; it's possible. #ManCandy

Perhaps your guy is so stuck in a style rut that he's been wearing the same look since college, and he's hell-bent on keeping that old pair of khakis until they have holes. If this sounds like your guy, I am about to change your world. I'm going to teach you how to shop for your man and help him look like a million bucks. In this chapter, you're going to learn exactly how to upgrade your man's wardrobe and get him to actually wear the new clothes (and enjoy looking great!).

WHAT ARE WE WORKING WITH?

OKAY, STEP ONE: Remember when you pulled everything out of your closet, sorted through your wardrobe, and got rid of the stuff you don't wear anymore? Well, put on your thinking cap and repeat what you did in Chapter Two—but this time, do it for your guy.

Once you've emptied out his closet, divide everything into three piles. The first pile is for donations—you can donate items to Goodwill, Out of the Closet, or you can even do some research and donate his clothes to a sober-living facility for men. The second pile is for items that you are just tossing, and the last pile is for items you're keeping. And before you get rid of something, make sure you run it by him first.

When you're weeding things out, it's important to be thorough but fair. Yes, you can get rid of the white shirts with the pit stains, suits that have been dry-cleaned to death, pants that haven't fit in years, those ugly sweaters his mother gave him, and items that are moth-eaten, but if you throw away his favorite sports jersey, it's kind of like you're throwing away his adult blankie. Don't do it! Even if he's never going to set foot on the field or the court again, let him have this dreams. The same goes for sentimental items that you know he'd freak out about if they disappeared, like his high school varsity letter jacket.

THE (MINI) MAN CLOSET MAKEOVER

STEP TWO: Give his closet a mini makeover. You don't need to go to town the way you did with yours because he honestly won't notice, but clean it out, get some new hangers and storage bins if you need to, and organize things. Hang his dress shirts together, then suits, then pants, then jackets. If needed, add a light, and if you want to really push it, the scent of cedar chips is masculine and won't impose on his masculinity. Make it easier for him (and for you) to find things.

GETTING DOWN TO BASICS

By clearing out your husband's (or boyfriend's) closet, you've begun the process of paring his wardrobe down. Remember, he's probably only wearing 20 percent of those pieces anyway! The items that are left should be the pieces he always wears, he likes, and that fit him well. If you did your job thoroughly, and I know you did, you have some basic items to play with, and now you can build him a stylish, functional wardrobe that meets all his needs.

Note: The idea here isn't to turn your guy into a clone, but to create a concise wardrobe of fundamental basics that I believe every man needs. There are many things you love about your guy—especially his uniqueness.

He probably has some fun pieces that help showcase his personality and separate him from the herd. For example, if he loves his Hawaiian shirts, or rock-star T's—that's awesome, let him have his fun. But this list is to ensure that when it's most important, he has those key items that will help him dress appropriately for every occasion.

LZ'S GUIDE TO THE MALE WARDROBE

CLOTHES:

- **TWO-PIECE SUITS IN BLACK, NAVY, AND GRAY**: How many suits your husband is going to need will depend on his lifestyle and tastes. If he wears a suit to work every day, then it would be best if he has at least three to five. If he only wears a suit for special occasions, then he only needs one, possibly two. If that's the case, make it black—as you know, black is the most versatile color.

- **NAVY BLAZER.**

- **DRESS SHIRTS**: He should have a couple of white dress shirts and a few dress shirts with color and pattern such as powder blue, light gray, and the all-important pinstripe.

- **FLAT-FRONT CHINOS IN KHAKI, GRAY, AND NAVY**: Repeat after me: NO PLEATS.

- **TWO PAIRS OF JEANS**: One dark denim for dressier occasions and the other his jean of choice.

- **SEVERAL POLO SHIRTS**: In colors that range from black to red to a striped rugby style. I love www.lacoste.com.

- **A FEW WHITE T-SHIRTS**: You can get these in packets of three from Hanes or Calvin Klein.

- **UNDERWEAR**: Is your guy a brief or boxer guy? It really is a personal preference, except when it comes to a special occasion, and I highly suggest that every man wear a pair of briefs under a suit to keep the lines classic and clean.

- **TWO DENIM SHIRTS**: One distressed and casual and the other a dressier chambray.

- **A BLACK PULLOVER** in cotton or wool.

- **A NAVY CARDIGAN** in cotton or wool.

- **BASIC CARGO SHORTS** in khaki or navy.

- **SWIM TRUNKS** in whatever style he likes.

- **A BLACK OR BROWN LEATHER BOMBER JACKET.**

- **A CLASSIC BLACK WOOL TOP COAT.**

- **A BASIC RAINCOAT** in black or tan.

- **A TAN WINDBREAKER.**

SHOES:

- **BASIC LOAFERS** in brown and black leather.

- **A BLACK LEATHER LACE-UP**: Can be worn to work and on special occasions (this should be a higher-end shoe if your budget allows).

- **DRIVING SHOES.**

- **ANKLE BOOTS** in black or brown, or biker boots.

- WORKOUT SHOES.

- A PAIR OF FLIP-FLOPS OR SANDALS: For summer.

ACCESSORIES:

- TIES: This will depend on his work situation and lifestyle. If your guy is a 9-5-type man, he will need an assortment of ties in different widths, colors, and textures.

- TIE BARS: This is a personal choice but it does add a vintage feel when paired with a skinny tie.

- BELT: A reversible brown/black leather belt with a matte-finish metal buckle.

- HANDKERCHIEFS: For his lapel. You can do a basic white or infuse some color and pattern.

- SOCKS: In black and an assortment of colors. Traditionally, the color of your socks should match the color of your trousers (unless you're wearing jeans, in which case they should match the color of your shoe).

- CUFFLINKS: For dress shirts, French cuffs are always classy.

- SATCHEL: He should really have a leather satchel or messenger bag. I feel the briefcase is passé. If your guy has to carry a laptop to work, get him a bag with some style.

- EYEWEAR: A cool pair of sunglasses. (PS: When it comes to eyewear, personally I love to wear Sama frames. Designer Sheila Vance is a pioneer when it comes to designing eyewear that's truly unique and will become a signature staple of one's wardrobe. Check them out at www.samaeyewear.net.)

IF YOU WIN THE LOTTERY, ADD:

- A HIGH-END SUIT FROM A LABEL LIKE TOM FORD OR BRUNELLO CUCINELLI.
- A NAVY CASHMERE SPORT COAT FROM RALPH LAUREN BLACK LABEL.
- A WATCH FROM ROLEX, TAG HEUER, OR BREITLING.
- CUSTOM-MADE SHOES. Since men's shoes rarely go out of style, a pair of custom-made shoes will last a lifetime. The Left Shoe Company (www.leftshoecompany.com) in Los Angeles is a great source for this ultimate in luxury, as is Leffot (http://leffot.com) in New York City.

"FASHION IS NOT NECESSARILY ABOUT LABELS. IT'S NOT ABOUT BRANDS. IT'S ABOUT SOMETHING ELSE THAT COMES FROM WITHIN YOU."

—RALPH LAUREN

Okay, ladies, take a deep breath. As with your wardrobe, you do not have to go out and buy all these pieces in one day. This is just your guide that will always be there for you as a reference. Buy what you can, when you can.

Now that you know my must-haves for your man's wardrobe, let's break down your guy's shape.

NAME THAT BODY TYPE

Of course, before you go shopping, you need to know your man's body type. Does this sound familiar? You've identified your own shape and now it's time to do the same for your man.

THE REGULAR JOE

If your guy's suit size falls between a 38 regular and a 41 regular, he's the average American size. And that, of course, means that you've got the most options when it comes to shopping.

Most things are going to fit and most things are going to look good on your guy. But do you want your guy to look average, or do you want him to look great? I thought so. And that means I'm going to climb on my soapbox again and bring up one of my favorite topics: tailoring. I haven't mentioned it for, oh, 10 pages, so you knew it was coming up. And in many cases, tailoring is included in the price of men's clothes.

THE NAPOLEON

Napoleon was one of the greatest military strategists of all time. He was also a short man. If your guy is less than 5'8" tall, he's considered to be short. Now, this is a hard thing for guys to accept, despite the fact that twice as many men fall into this category.

If he's shorter, he's going to need a shorter inseam and a shorter rise or his pants are going to look too big. Up top, he's going to need his sleeves short-ened. He does not want to look like a little boy who's wearing dad's jacket.

With the Napoleon body type, you want to avoid anything that breaks the line of the body up. Stay away from horizontal stripes, contrasting blocks of color, and high collars. And if your man wants to be elevated from a few inches to many inches, step on over to www.tallmenshoes.com and add a little height and confidence to your man's size.

THE SIX-PACK GUY

There are six-pack abs and then there are six-pack abs. Here I refer to the ones that come from ingesting a six-pack of beer on a regular basis. Ladies, there's no nice way to say this but if your guy has a belly, then he falls into my Six-Pack Guy category. The best way to handle this body shape is to balance his top and bottom so that the tummy isn't the first thing the eye goes to. He's not going to look skinny but he'll look like he's big and powerful rather than like a guy with a gut.

Stay away from anything that clings, like thin knits. Stay within a one-color family rather than ones that break up the line of the body with blocks of color. Up top, look for jackets with shoulder pads to create the illusion of bigger shoulders. Down below, go for wide-legged pants to create the illusion of a wide base. Stay away from low-rise jeans that sit below the gut and emphasize it.

Remember, *big* shouldn't mean *sloppy*. If your guy's waist is big, he's going to have to get pants that are proportionately bigger. Have the inseam taken in and the hem taken up to avoid looking baggy all over. Same with his shirts—to fit his girth, he's probably going to size up. So when he wears one untucked (a great way to camouflage a tummy), make sure it doesn't hug his body or hit him at mid-thigh.

THE ATHLETE

If your guy is the athletic type, you already know he's got a killer body. What you may not know is that just because he's got a killer body doesn't mean he's going to be easy to dress. Athletes tend to have bigger shoulders and necks, bigger glutes (translation: he's got a great butt) and smaller waists. It's like their proportions are exaggerated, which means that, yes, you guessed it, they're going to need help from our old friend Mr. Tailor.

For the Athlete, I would stay away from jackets with padded shoulders since he's already, in effect, got them. Have pants taken in at the waist and the rise if needed. Shirts may need to be taken in at the waist too. And just because he's got good legs doesn't mean he should be wearing super-skinny pants. The bottom of the body needs to be a counterpoint to the top or he's going to look out of proportion. Classic-fit pants are a better bet.

THE LONG AND LANKY

Do people continually ask your guy what the weather is like up there? Are his arms so long that when he puts his arm around you at the movies it reaches across the shoulders of the person sitting next to you?

If you've answered yes to any of these questions, your guy is long and lanky. The biggest challenge in dressing a man with this body type is to prevent him from looking like a teenage boy who's not yet grown into his height. Horizontal stripes give the illusion of a broader chest. If his legs are skinny, look for pants and jeans with a little width to them to counteract that

Dress shirts are often a problem for taller guys. If you want to invest the money, specialty shirtmakers like Thomas Pink (www.thomaspink.com) make long lengths. Big-and-tall shops are great for guys who are tall and wide; if your guy is tall and skinny, you could shop for dress shirts there and have the torso altered by a tailor.

THE SUPERSIZED

"Hey, big guy." "How much can you bench press?" "Whoa!" If your husband gets these comments all the time, he's Supersized—big, tall, and a whole lotta man. When he's Supersized, he can be in proportion or he might have a tummy. Either way, he's larger than life. If he's in proportion, the key is to make sure that everything fits or he'll look sloppy and ungainly. Check sleeve lengths and make sure the crotch of his pants doesn't hang down to his knees.

Big-and-tall shops are key. Two favorites are www.foundrybigandtall.com and www.rochesterbigandtall.com.

SHOPPING FOR THE MAN

Now it's time to shop. Yay! First, I want to address suits because they are usually the biggest expense for a guy. I firmly believe that every man should have a quality black two-piece suit and here's why: it will get him through weddings, funerals, special dinners, and even black-tie events.

If he only wears a suit a couple of times a year, you still want it to last because he's clearly not the kind of guy who likes to go out and buy suits. It's easy to find an affordable, quality suit. There's always some kind of suit special at places like the Men's Wearhouse (www.menswearhouse.com), Century 21 (www.c21stores.com), or Jos. A. Bank (www.josbank.com). They all carry short, regular, tall, and larger sizes.

SUITING UP: HOW TO KNOW WHEN A SUIT FITS

Buying a well-made suit is a major investment, so you want it to fit right. The most versatile suit a man can own is a two-piece, two-button black suit. A suit should be close-fitting but not tight. The jacket should be as wide as your guy's shoulders. The shoulder fit is super important to get right from the get-go because it's an expensive pain in the butt to fix. If the shoulders fit, a tailor can help you with everything else. LZ note: When he's being fitted for the proper suit, write down all the measurements the tailor takes—jacket size, dress-shirt collar and sleeves, waist and inseam—and then use this information when you go shopping for him, whether it's to update his wardrobe or when you're buying him gifts for special occasions.

"I CAN GO ALL OVER THE WORLD WITH JUST THREE OUTFITS: A BLUE BLAZER AND GREY FLANNEL PANTS, A GREY FLANNEL SUIT, AND BLACK TIE."

—PIERRE CARDIN

SHOPPING STRATEGY

Here are some of my favorite places to shop for men from head to toe.

- **BROOKS BROTHERS** (www.brooksbrothers.com): An American classic, Brooks Brothers is the home of the perfect white button-down. Plus they have classic wardrobe pieces for every man's closet.

- **BURLINGTON** (www.burlingtoncoatfactory.com): An oldie but a goodie, this is a great place to shop for suits, shirts, slacks, and, of course, coats.

- **JOHN VARVATOS** (www.johnvarvatos.com): Personal favorite. #RockStar

- **HUGO BOSS** (www.hugoboss.com): Another favorite. #MovieStar

- **JCPENNEY** (www.jcpenney.com): Features their own private labels that are affordable and extremely stylish.

- **MR PORTER** (www.mrporter.com): When you want to splurge, Mr Porter will help you do it in style. The menswear branch of Net-a-Porter has an incredible selection. And their tips and suggestions are a fantastic resource.

- **SHORT MEN STYLE** (www.shortmenstyle.com): This retailer is dedicated to outfitting the shorter man and they stock a full array of pants, shirts, and jackets.

- **ROCHESTER BIG & TALL** (www.rochesterclothing.com): Another excellent resource for our big and tall guys.

- **THE FOUNDRY** (www.foundrybigandtall.com): The Foundry is dedicated to the big guy. Sizes go up to 8XL.

SURVIVAL OF THE FITTEST:

LZ'S TOP 5 TIPS FOR SHOPPING WITH YOUR MAN

Most of the time, you're probably shopping for your guy rather than with him. But when you absolutely need him there, here are my tips for making it a positive experience.

1. **SET A TIMELINE**: If he knows your shopping expedition is only going to take two hours, he won't feel like he's trapped for the entire day.

2. **SCOUT IT OUT**: Before you take him shopping, take a quick scouting trip. Visit the store and have the sales clerk set aside some pieces you'd like him to try on. This means you won't lose his attention as soon as you walk in the door. Make it fun. Make it fast.

3. **MULTITASK**: While he's trying on the first batch of items, you hit the floor and look for more. When he comes out, give the look he's tried on a thumbs up or down, and before he goes back in the dressing room, show him the new pieces you pulled, and have him try on the one he likes the best first. This will get him involved, and make him feel like he's in control.

4. **STROKE HIS EGO**: Be very complimentary of the pieces that look good on him, and tell him why. The idea is to encourage him with words like sexy, hot, or even yummy . . . so you'll put a smile on his face and make this experience fun.

5. **BUILD IN A REWARD**: Make sure there's a reward for him at the end of the day, whether that's his favorite dinner or his favorite dessert (which is you, of course!).

CHOOSE YOUR MOMENTS WISELY

The key is to wait until the right time presents itself, and that means not when he's watching football. Maybe when you're getting ready to go out, show him a new shirt and suggest he try it on first before he gets dressed for the night. Make it fun. Be flirty. Tell him how great he looks. Pour it on thick and hot, ladies. Remember, you're trying to change his world here. It won't happen without some effort and some mild manipulation. (C'mon, I know this won't be the first time.)

HERE COMES THE GROOMING

What women call beauty, men call grooming, but it's essentially the same thing. Deep down inside, men want to look nice; but to get most men to commit to even a basic skincare routine can be challenging. Again, baby steps. This is exactly why I asked my friend and groomer to the stars, Benjamin Thigpen, to give you his 411 on the perfect skin for your man.

BENJAMIN THIGPEN'S CALLING CARD

WEBSITE: WWW.ABTP.COM/HAIR/BENJAMIN-THIGPEN

FACEBOOK: WWW.FACEBOOK.COM/BENJAMIN.THIGPEN

TWITTER & INSTAGRAM: @BENJAMINTHIGPEN

CELEBRITIES: BRUCE WILLIS, MARC JACOBS, CHRIS NOTH, NATE BERKUS,

ANDY COHEN, STEVE BUSCEMI, ALAN CUMMING, JUST TO NAME A FEW

KEEP IT CLEAN

Guys should wash their faces at least twice a day. If they're outside a lot working or sweating, they could even do it three times. My favorite face wash for guys is Recipe for Men Facial Cleanser. It's mild but deep cleansing and it helps to reduce breakouts. Cleanse, moisturize, protect, that's my theory! Whether their skin is dry, oily, or combo, they need a good non-clogging moisturizer with an SPF of no less than 15. Once a month every guy should exfoliate with a very light scrub on the face and neck to remove dead skin. I personally exfoliate my face, neck, upper chest, and back.

In the summer months when I am soaking up the sun, I always use a moisturizer with a high SPF to protect against sun damage. I also recommend that everyone visit the doc at least once a year to check for precancerous lesions. Better safe than sorry!

GET A CLOSE SHAVE

The first step to a close shave for any guy is cleansing the skin in warm water with a moisturizing face wash to open the pores and soften the stubble.

Next, he needs a thick shaving gel, preferably moisturizing, that should be rubbed on the face and neck, and left for a minute or two to further soften the beard. Only a sharp razor (i.e., sharp enough to cut the hairs with one stroke) should be used.

Shaving should be done in the direction of hair growth (for most guys, that's down). The blade should be rinsed in warm water after every stroke. If stubble is still visible, go over the area again, this time at an angle.

After rinsing the face with cold water to close the pores, he will want to use a very light moisturizer.

Like I said before, each person is different—your guy may find an electric razor works better. For other men, the heat from the machine makes their skin red. Whatever the routine, he needs to feel comfortable. If your guy has redness or breakouts, then most likely he needs a new routine or new products.

LZ'S MAN MUST-HAVES

Here's a quick list of some of the products I always use that work for me.

- SKINCARE PRODUCTS FROM THE FACE PLACE (WWW.FACEPLACE.COM)

- DR. BRANDT UV 30 SPF HIGHT PROTECTION FACE (HTTP://WWW.DRBRANDTSKINCARE.COM)

- CLARISONIC SKIN CLEANER (WWW.CLARISONIC.COM)

- MENAJI 911 EYE GEL (WWW.MENAJI.COM)

- HYDRO COOL FIRMING EYE GELS FROM SKYN ICEI AND (WWW.SKYNICEI AND.COM)

- JACK BLACK BEARD LUBE (WWW.GETJACKBLACK.COM)

- BLISS BODY BUTTER (WWW.BLISSWORLD.COM)

A HAIRY SITUATION

Yes, hair is manly and can be sexy, but too much can get grizzly and gross. Much of the time, men don't care about it, but if it bothers you, then help your man maintain it by trimming, waxing, shaving, plucking, or even using a laser. It's a delicate conversation, but so worth it. Just remember to be kind and considerate, not condescending or nagging.

If it's nose or ear hair that's out of control, gently tell him that you've noticed a few stray hairs and suggest he trim them, or ask him to have them taken care of at his next haircut. Just don't let him pluck, especially around the nose, because that can lead to a serious infection.

When it comes to the unibrow, I'm guilty as charged. Yes, I once had a unibrow. Consider this our bonding moment. But at a certain point, I took care of it and so should your man. Use all your powers of persuasion for this one and remember to tread lightly.

One of the most sensitive topics of discussion for a man is hair loss. There are those who are blessed with a full head of hair their entire lives, but that is not the norm. Male pattern baldness affects millions of men; it's extremely common, but it can still be very damaging to a man's ego.

There are treatment options available, including Vitamin B, Keratin Enhance, Rogaine, and Propecia. Another route is to invest in a hair-restoration procedure, which can set you back financially when properly done. Or he can just let nature take its course and as his hair thins, you should encourage him to keep it cut short. My final thoughts: no comb overs and no toupees. Period. Finally, in an attempt to hold on to their youth, many men will cover their grays by coloring their hair with boxed products from the local drugstore. Once again, the intention is good but the results can be disastrous, so it's up to you to help him find his way to a salon to have it done professionally, or help him embrace the gray and transition into a sexy, silver fox.

SHOW OF HANDS (AND FEET)

Gnarly paws and hooves are the worst. Be assured, there's nothing emasculating about a guy getting his nails done, and if my dad could do it, so can your man. A gift certificate for a mani-pedi makes a fantastic Father's Day present and it will come just in time for summer. If he's still resistant, then the next time you go away for the weekend, book a spa day for the two of you. Get massages, facials, mani-pedis—the works. Once he's experienced the pampering, he'll be hooked.

"THE BEST SMELL IN THE WORLD IS THAT MAN THAT YOU LOVE."
—JENNIFER ANISTON

TOP FIVE TAKEAWAYS FROM LZ'S EIGHTH COMMANDMENT

ONE DEFINE YOUR MAN'S BODY TYPE BEFORE YOU GO SHOPPING FOR HIM.

TWO WHEN IT COMES TO ENHANCING YOUR MAN'S WARDROBE, ADD NEW PIECES SLOWLY OVER TIME AND WHEN YOUR BUDGET ALLOWS.

THREE DON'T ASK HIM TO TRY THINGS ON WHEN HE'S NOT IN THE MOOD (OR WATCHING FOOTBALL). CHOOSE YOUR MOMENTS CAREFULLY.

FOUR MAKE A LIST OF YOUR GUY'S SIZES, FAVORITE COLORS, DESIGNERS, AND NEEDS TO MAKE SHOPPING FOR HIM EASIER.

FIVE BE SENSITIVE WHEN ADDRESSING YOUR MAN'S GROOMING NEEDS.

9

THOU SHALT DRESS
AS THOUGH
EVERY DAY IS A
SPECIAL OCCASION

"FASHION IS VERY IMPORTANT. IT IS LIFE-ENHANCING AND, LIKE EVERYTHING THAT GIVES PLEASURE, IT IS WORTH DOING WELL."

—VIVIENNE WESTWOOD

Every day of your life is a gift and we've got to appreciate today for the beautiful gift that it is. In fact, I want you to get in the mindset of thinking of each and every day as a special occasion, and I want you to reflect that in every way, from how you treat others, to the choices you make, and the way you dress. And, in all reality, those things don't take that much effort: a little goes a long way.

Now, you're probably asking what being kind to others has to do with special occasion dressing. I'm glad you asked. As Annie so famously proclaimed, "You're never fully dressed without a smile," and if that smile comes from a place deep inside of you, a place of love, caring, and kindness, then it comes across as genuine and . . . wait for it . . . beautiful. Kindness shines through you like a bright light, making you absolutely beam from the inside out. Give a little love, look a little lovelier.

Furthermore, you are worthy of looking fabulous, not just for certain events, but each and every day of the week. Think about all those outfits you bought because you were going somewhere significant—a friend's wedding, a christening, an anniversary dinner. Every time you open your closet door and look at them, you feel good. You remember how gorgeous you looked in them, the compliments you received, the great time you had.

So here's my question: Why do you wear those beautiful pieces only for special events? Why do you only wear your Sunday best to church when you could incorporate some of those pieces into your daily routine? Why can't there be something extraordinary about every ordinary day? Whether you're going to work, brunching with the girls, or on a date, it's easier than you think to turn every day into a #SpecialOccasion.

NO TIME LIKE THE PRESENT!

YOU CAN MAKE TODAY A SPECIAL OCCASION, STARTING RIGHT NOW. START SMALL. PULL OUT THAT BEAUTIFUL SWEATER, THE ONE THAT MAKES PEOPLE SAY, "YOU LOOK GREAT!" AND PUT IT ON. OR, PUT ON SOME LIPSTICK BEFORE YOU HEAD TO THE SUPERMARKET. INSTEAD OF WEARING YOUR FLATS, THROW ON A PAIR OF SHOES THAT MAKES YOU FEEL SEXY . . . IT'S THOSE SIMPLE NUANCES THAT WILL CHANGE HOW YOU FEEL AND YOUR DAY. BE GOOD TO YOURSELF AND SHOW YOURSELF A LITTLE RESPECT—YOU'VE EARNED IT.

"KNOWING YOUR 'CHARACTER' IS THE KEY TO CULTIVATING YOUR STYLE. WITH THE RIGHT CLOTHES, YOU CAN BE WHOMEVER YOU WANT TO BE. AND YOU CAN CHANGE YOUR 'CHARACTER' FROM DAY TO DAY, DEPENDING ON YOUR NEEDS AND WHIMS."
—JANIE BRYANT, COSTUME DESIGNER AND AUTHOR

LZ'S TAKE TEN IN THE PM

The easiest way to dress as if each day is a special occasion is to take 10 extra minutes in the evening to plan out the outfit you're going to wear the next day. Think about where you're going, what you need to do, and the look you want to create (see, now you're thinking like a stylist—bravo!). Find a place where you can display your look, whether it's on a bed, on a couch, or whatever, and lay it out, including jewelry. This gives you time to see if anything needs to be steamed, pressed, or mended, or if your shoes need to be polished. No more rushed, frantic mornings for you.

Let's say you have an important business meeting in the morning and you really want to make a style statement. Pull out your basic two-piece black suit, but instead of the pants, you choose your pencil skirt and then think about the details that elevate it. For example, you can bump it up a notch with textured hose, which will show off your legs, and then add your sexy pumps that you usually save for Saturday night. Instead of the crisp, white dress shirt, opt for a brightly colored silk blouse and then layer on those strands of pearls that you'd usually wear for a night at the theater. And voila! You've taken some of those pieces you normally wear only for special events and incorporated them into your daily life.

CUT TO: Morning. Rise and shine! Your outfit is already planned so you have a little extra time to do something different with your hair, experiment with a new lip color, or try on a new fragrance. (The great Coco Chanel once said, "A woman who doesn't wear perfume has no future," which was Coco's dramatic way of saying she isn't prepared for any good thing that might happen to her.)

FULL-FIGURED AND FAB

Did you know that the average American woman is a size 14/16? True story! But if you're one of my fuller-figured femme fatales, I know very well that getting dressed for any occasion can be frustrating and quite an emotional experience. You want to look stylish, but the options are so limited. I know that, because I have been in the trenches (dressing rooms) with plus-size women and I've witnessed firsthand the struggles they go through. I was the official, national spokesperson for Lane Bryant for seven glorious years. During that time, I traveled around the country doing in-store appearances and makeovers on curvy girls and I helped show them how to celebrate their size.

Now, there was a time when *Lane Bryant* and a handful of specialty shops were the only stores that catered to women size 14 and up. I'm here to tell you that things have changed! Due to the high demand, more designers in the past 10 years have really embraced the fuller-figured woman and are now creating clothing that's on trend and in style.

Let me add one more layer to this story. One of my closest friends, Lenora, is 5'5" and a beautiful size 14/16 with curves in all the right places. (Curves, by the way, that her husband is obsessed with.) Now, I've taken Lenora shopping many times and I know what a struggle it is for her to find clothes that fit. It does take a little time, but now that I've got her shopping like a stylist, she has the vision to pick out the pieces she knows will be right for her and she has learned what the proper tailoring can do. By the way, she's an absolute knockout.

So, every time I tell you to have your items tailored to fit, don't roll your eyes and think that doesn't apply to you. It does! No matter what your size, you don't have to wear muumuus and you can look gorgeous for all of your special occasions.

"OVER THE YEARS I HAVE LEARNED THAT WHAT IS IMPORTANT IN A DRESS IS THE WOMAN WHO IS WEARING IT."

—YVES SAINT LAURENT

WHEN YOU'RE CELEBRATING A SPECIAL OCCASION

I'm talking about family weddings, christenings, anniversaries, bar mitzvahs—the all-important red-carpet events of your life. These are special occasions and you know what that means: photos, photos, and more photos. Sweetheart, those pictures are going to be around forever. When you look at them 20 years from now, your first thought should be, "what a great night," not "yikes, what was I wearing?" So, trust me when I say this is not the time to experiment with trends. Stay classic with your choices. Think timeless when it comes to your outfit, your hair, and your makeup. We all have those event photos that make us cringe. What were we thinking? And put in a little extra prep time. It's the style equivalent of "measure twice, cut once."

One week before the big day, try everything on: dress, shoes, shapewear, hair, makeup, accessories . . . the works. Take a look at yourself in the mirror. How does it all work? If something doesn't fit well, doesn't match, or is uncomfortable, you've got time to fix it. I'm also going to suggest you pull out that camera again and take a photo of yourself at this point. Sometimes you won't see it in the mirror but it will show up in the photo. (You may think your bra isn't visible under your top, but photos don't lie, and they might even show your bra looking like a neon sign under your blouse!) Have your husband or a friend shine a flashlight behind you and take another photo. This is a good way to see whether anything's too sheer.

The idea is to troubleshoot anything that can go wrong so when you're dressing for the event, you can just enjoy the process and look forward to celebrating with your friends and family.

"A DRESS SHOULD NOT ONLY LOOK FABULOUS BUT
ALSO MAKE A WOMAN FEEL GLAMOROUS."

DAVID MEISTER

HOW TO PERFECTLY POSE FOR PICS

NOW THAT YOU LOOK LIKE A MOVIE STAR, HERE'S HOW TO POSE LIKE ONE. IF YOU'RE POSING WITH SOMEONE ELSE, DON'T PUT YOUR ARM OVER THEIR SHOULDER OR ELSE YOU'LL LOOK LIKE THE HUNCHBACK OF NOTRE DAME. INSTEAD, PUT YOUR ARM AROUND THEIR WAIST. IF YOU'RE ON YOUR OWN, THE BEAUTY QUEEN POSE NEVER FAILS: TURN SO THAT YOU'RE FACING THREE-QUARTERS TOWARD THE CAMERA, PUT YOUR HAND ON YOUR HIP TO MAKE YOUR WAIST LOOK SMALLER, AND KEEP YOUR WEIGHT ON YOUR BACK FOOT. DON'T FIDGET. TAKE A DEEP BREATH (IN THROUGH THE NOSE, OUT THROUGH THE MOUTH), LICK YOUR LIPS, AND SMILE. AND YES, AUNTIE RIMA, THAT MEANS YOU!

JUST WHAT IS "COCKTAIL" ATTIRE?

Because not all celebrations are created equal, let me break them down for you. Luckily, the invitation usually gives us a clue as to what to expect.

THE SEMI-FORMAL

This is the most flexible type of occasions. Men wear suits and women wear dresses or even dressy pants suits. But don't opt for a work suit unless you take it to a whole other level with rich silky fabric tops, some statement jewelry, and some sexy special occasion shoes. Look for fabrics like silk, velvet, and brocade. Don't show too much cleavage or leg—this is neither the time nor the place, ladies, no matter how impressive you think they are or how much you love them. If the dress is understated, bring out your bling; if it's embellished, keep the jewelry simple. This is definitely the time to get out your heels. They can be simple pumps or a strappy slingback. For a handbag, I like a clutch for all dressier occasion. Bags with straps don't look as polished.

COCKTAIL ATTIRE

The rules for cocktail and semi-formal are similar, but you can get away with a little more for cocktail because it's in the evening. So while you might wear a pastel dress to a semi-formal daytime wedding, for a cocktail event, you can go for a rich jewel tone that's knee length and beaded. Again, if your dress has an abundance of details, keep the jewelry quiet—maybe some hoops or a simple bracelet. If your dress is toned down, you can pile on a little more. Men should be in dark suits with dress shirts and ties.

BLACK TIE

For guys, it's easy: If the invitation says black tie, they should wear a tuxedo with a black bow tie, or they can get away with a regular tie as long as it's black. For women, this is the time to pull out all the stops and think red-carpet royalty. You can wear a full-length evening gown or, depending on the style, a three-quarter-length dress. Jewelry should be the best you own or some fab affordable knock-offs. And if you don't own, you can rent—see the list of websites in Chapter Seven: Thou Shalt Shop Wisely (and Online!) for ideas on where to rent major bling. Your heels should be high and coordinate with your dress, and for my ladies that prefer a lower heel, every single shoe designer has created evening shoe options that are just as stylish and comfortable.

WHITE TIE

This is the most formal of occasions and really only refers to an event that takes place after 6 p.m. Men wear a black tailcoat and trousers, a white waistcoat, a starched white shirt, and a white bow tie. For women, a ball gown is the traditional choice. Unless your life is a constant round of white-tie events, this is not an item I recommend spending a lot of money on. Once again, I suggest renting a top designer gown, which will not only save you money but make you look like a million bucks. How many of us have a reason to keep a ball gown in our closets, after all? Cocktail dresses and three-quarter dresses are not appropriate for white tie—they're just not formal enough for this type of occasion. If you're being very traditional, long white gloves are worn and are removed for dinner. Bracelets are worn over the gloves. Again, your jewelry should be the best you have and renting is a perfectly respectable option. A chic evening shoe, a clutch, and some sort of wrap are the only other accessories you need.

LEAVING ON A JET PLANE

This chapter is all about special occasion dressing, and I fully believe we can bring a chic style to every life opportunity that is presented to us—whether at work, play, and even traveling.

When you're at home, you have your amazing wardrobe right at your finger-tips. But when you travel, you have to be more precise and selective when building your weekend, week-long, or extended trip wardrobe. And on top of that, you want to choose pieces that make you feel special.

WHAT TO WEAR IN THE AIR

Yes, I know you want to be comfortable when flying. I do, too. But that doesn't mean I'm going to wear my pajamas. There is nothing "special occasion" about PJs. (My brother Gregory, on the other hand . . .)

That said, when you're going to be walking through airports and then sitting in one place for hours at a time, comfort is of the utmost importance. For one thing, you never know how long you're going to be in those clothes. So do yourself a favor and wear something with a little stretch, such as jeans with a bit of Lycra, a loose-fitting top, and another layer to keep you warm. Instead of wrapping yourself up in the same blanket everyone else has used, invest in a little luxury and buy a cashmere throw or an oversized scarf (FYI, I found some great inexpensive choices at www.overstock.com). Avoid wearing a sweater that you need to pull over your head; it just destroys your hair.

> "DRESS SHABBILY AND THEY REMEMBER THE DRESS;
> DRESS IMPECCABLY AND THEY REMEMBER THE WOMAN."
> —COCO CHANEL

Choose comfortable shoes that are easy to take on and off because you know you'll have to take them off at security. For safety reasons and for hygiene, I don't recommend flip-flops for flying. If you're not wearing socks, keep a clean pair in your handbag so you can slip them on before security because you don't want to have to walk through barefoot.

Also don't overload yourself with accessories and metal items that you'll just have to take off at security. Keep those items in your bag and accessorize once you're through security. It's easier for you, a courtesy to everyone else, and makes you a fashionably friendly frequent flier. I definitely see an upgrade in your future.

WHAT'S IN YOUR BAG?

Now, when it comes to travel, some of the hardest decisions to make are what to take on the trip. I fly frequently, and I have packing down to a science. Or maybe it's an art. Whatever you want to call it, I do it all the time and I know what works and what doesn't. So listen up, kids.

LZ'S TRIED-AND-TRUE PACKING TIPS

1. **SIZE MATTERS.** Choose a size-appropriate suitcase and be strategic about what you bring.

2. **KNOW THE WEATHER WHERE YOU'RE GOING.** Check the weather online in advance and it will give you a guideline for what to pack.

3. **CHOOSE A COLOR AND STICK WITH IT.** When you travel, stick with one neutral color, such as black, navy, or gray, and then brighten it up with layering pieces such as scarves and other accessories. This means everything works together.

4. **PACK MORE TOPS THAN BOTTOMS.** Solid-color jeans, skirts, and pants can be worn more than once, but tops don't always have that kind of life span. Plus, bottoms are heavier and take up more room than tops. Speaking of weight, wear your heaviest piece, such as a coat, on the plane and save yourself the trouble of packing it.

5.   **PLAN AHEAD.** Lay all your outfits out on the bed before you put them in the suitcase and see what goes with what. You can take pictures of each outfit with accessories and interchange them on your phone. This way you won't forget what you have once you arrive at your destination and have an early morning meeting while you're still jet-lagged.

"YOU CAN HAVE ANYTHING YOU WANT IN LIFE IF YOU DRESS FOR IT."
—EDITH HEAD,
EIGHT-TIME ACADEMY AWARD®-WINNING COSTUME DESIGNER

TAKE THIS, LEAVE THAT

When it comes to dressing like each day is a special occasion, women tend to opt for their very best jewelry because it makes them feel glamorous. However, when you're traveling, I suggest leaving your expensive jewelry at home. I have too many friends who have lost their expensive pieces. Costume jewelry is fine for travel and if you lose it, you won't be heartbroken.

Always make sure you have one pair of shoes that will stand up to rain or other extreme weather conditions. While you're at it, don't forget to pack a small umbrella and a foldable, lightweight raincoat. If you've bought clothes especially for your vacation, test them out at home before debuting them. You don't want to leave the hotel for a day of sightseeing and find out that your new white pants are see-through or your sundress requires a different bra.

I invested in a portable steamer a few years ago and it was the smartest $25 I've ever spent. It takes up very little room, works much better than the iron in your hotel room, and is more eco-conscious than running the shower to steam out your clothes. I use it at home, too, and I love it.

MAKE A LIST, CHECK IT TWICE

Over the years, I've learned the importance of a packing list. It's such a simple thing, but can help you avoid disaster. And if your luggage disappears or is stolen, then you have details of what needs to be claimed on insurance.

Sit down at your computer and make up a list of the important things you need to take with you at all times: your prescription medications, headache remedy, antacids, allergy pills, contact lens solutions, personal hygiene items, earplugs, eye mask, mouth guard, eyedrops, first-aid kit, hand sanitizer, disinfectant wipes, night-lights, extra pair of eyeglasses and sunglasses, power adapters, plastic travel-size bottles for your skincare, and whatever makes your life happier when you travel.

Keep an electronic copy and update as you need to. Before a trip, print it out and check off as you go along. It takes 98 percent of the stress out of packing. And my final trick is to always have natural charcoal tablets on hand in case of a stomach upset, especially when sampling exotic cuisine.

IF THE TRIP IS ALL BUSINESS

When you're traveling for business, you need to look neat and presentable. Of course, you do anyway because you've been listening to every word I say—thank you very much!

When I've got a quick two-day turnaround work trip, I wear my usual jeans, a dark T-shirt, and a zip knit hoodie for the plane, and I pack my suit. As soon as I arrive, I have it pressed at the hotel or at a local dry cleaner. Nothing says "I don't know what I'm doing" like a wrinkled suit.

Also, if you're traveling on business during the winter months, arrive at your meeting a few minutes early so you can take off your big coat and sweater, run a brush through your hair and check your makeup, and let your body adjust to the new inside temperature. Sweaty and disheveled is never a good look, kids. Along with your suit, bring a crisp, white dress shirt (plus a backup one) that you can wear with your dark jeans for off-duty dinner or drinks, a good leather handbag, a clutch for evening, a pair of pumps, and a couple knit tops that you can mix and match with your jeans and suit trousers. Knitwear, such as matte jersey, is a good option because it wrinkles less than wovens. Toss in some fun jewelry, your underwear and PJs, and your toiletries and you're good to go.

Also keep a pair of fuzzy socks in your suitcase for every trip. They're not as bulky as slippers but they keep your tootsies off of hotel room floors in the middle of the night.

TAKING A VACAY

Vacations are the real special occasions we want to travel for, so make sure you have what you need to make it the most fun possible. Bring your favorite items that always make you feel comfortable and look stylish. It's those little extras that make a trip special, like taking your best friend along with you. Some ladies pack things they never wear because they think they'll wear them for the first time while they're away. But in reality, it never happens. Stick with what you know and concentrate on enjoying your vacation.

IF YOU'RE GOING TO THE BEACH:

Think lighter, brighter colors, and lightweight fabrics such as cotton, gauze, and linen. For the ultimate vacation wardrobe, I suggest packing a couple of bathing suits in whatever style you like best, some sort of beach cover-up, be it a sarong or a caftan, sundresses, long flowing skirts, white jeans or white linen drawstring pants, a few floaty tops, espadrilles or sandals, sunglasses, flip-flops, a denim jacket, a big straw hat that is crushable for your suitcase, and a canvas beach bag that holds a lot but doesn't take up suitcase space or you can use as your extra item for carry-on. Also bring some fun, festive jewelry you can get for next to nothing at places like Forever 21 (www.forever21.com).

IF YOU'RE GOING SOMEPLACE COLD:

Think layers. Bring a few thin sweaters that you can double up on if you need to. Silk underwear (no, not that kind!) is a great insulator. I got mine at L.L. Bean (www.llbean.com). It keeps you warm without giving you that bulky look. Some basic items to bring are jeans, black trousers, turtlenecks, black tights and a pencil skirt for going out in the evenings, boots and/or comfortable walking shoes, a winter coat or leather jacket, and a tote. And no matter when you travel on vacation, ladies, don't forget your movie-star frames, a vibrant multicolored scarf in the season's hottest colors, and a bold lip color that will give every outfit that instant shot of glam.

TOP FIVE TAKEAWAYS FROM LZ'S NINTH COMMANDMENT

ONE   DRESS AND ACT LIKE EVERY DAY IS A GIFT, TRULY A SPECIAL OCCASION.

TWO   TAKE AN EXTRA 10 MINUTES AT THE END OF YOUR DAY TO PLAN AND PREP YOUR OUTFIT FOR THE NEXT MORNING.

THREE   WHEN DRESSING FOR A SPECIAL OCCASION, GIVE YOUR ENTIRE LOOK A RUN-THROUGH THE WEEK BEFORE.

FOUR   WHEN YOU TRAVEL, CHOOSE ONE DOMINANT COLOR AND ACCESSORIZE WITH BRIGHTER, TRENDIER PIECES.

FIVE   PACK SMART WHEN TRAVELING, AND KEEP A LIST OF EVERYTHING YOU'RE TAKING ON YOUR TRIP.

10

THOU SHALT
CREATE YOUR
OWN STYLE
COMMANDMENT

My Style Commandment

"A NEW DRESS DOESN'T GET YOU ANYWHERE. IT'S THE LIFE
YOU'RE LIVING IN THAT DRESS THAT MATTERS."

—DIANA VREELAND

■ Okay, kids, this is your tenth and final chapter, and guess what? You did it! You made it through nine of my commandments! I am incredibly proud of you, and it makes me so happy knowing that you have trusted me to be your guide on this powerful journey. You probably never imagined the changes you would be making when you picked up this book. You might have thought you were just going to learn how to dress, but this has been about so much more than just your wardrobe. Well, we've got one more commandment to cover, and this one is truly all about Y-O-U.

Before we get into the details, I want to give you a little head's up: I've talked to some of my gorgeous celebrity friends who happen to be timeless beauties and asked them to share with me what makes them feel sexy. You'll be inspired by what they had to say, and you'll find these sparkling jewels scattered throughout this chapter.

Now, the first part of this final commandment is to do a little reflecting. Remember how this journey started? Of course you do; how could you forget? You were standing naked in front of the mirror and I was asking you to take a long, hard look at yourself. It's not the kind of experience that can easily be put behind you (no pun intended . . . ha!). But if I've done my job and you've listened, taken notes, and put my suggestions into action, then the way you look at yourself now is not at all the way you looked at yourself before. Give yourself a round of applause! (Louder! Louder!)

"I BELIEVE SEXINESS IS A PURE STATE OF BEING. IT HAS NOTHING TO DO WITH WHAT YOU WEAR, BUT RATHER IT'S ABOUT HOW YOU FEEL ABOUT THE PERSON BENEATH THE CLOTHES."
—CARRIE ANN INABA, TV HOST AND CHOREOGRAPHER

A PICTURE IS WORTH (MORE THAN)
A THOUSAND WORDS

Here's an important exercise to really round out this experience for you: Do you remember back in the First Commandment when I asked you to take a "before" photo of yourself? Well, now it's time to take the "after" photo with your new and improved look. You've worked so hard for this, so make it special by getting all glammed up and dressed to kill. This is your makeover moment; this is *your* before and after.

Then, look at both photos and think about the journey you've been on. You, my dear, you look fantastic, and *you* did that! And I have to say, I would be beyond thrilled if you would be willing to share your before-and-after photos with me on my Facebook fan page: www.facebook.com/LAWRENCEZARIAN. It will also connect you with a community of women that are on the same journey. #StyleSupport

Okay, but let's take it one step further and actually play a little game of compare and contrast. There's a lot more in that photo than just a new skirt or pair of shoes. Isn't it amazing what can happen when you work on the inside *while* you transform the outside? You can feel and see the changes. Remember when you used to have those old, negative mental recordings, that awful inner commentary about yourself that you used to play over and over in your head? My sincere hope is that those are long gone! You've replaced those negative thoughts with new, positive recordings that reinforce your beauty and who you are. You were always beautiful; the only difference is that now you actually see it and *believe* it. Welcome to your party, gorgeous!

"WHAT MAKES ME FEEL SEXY? FEELING MY BOYFRIEND'S EYES ON ME AS I WALK OUT OF A ROOM."

—DONNA MILLS, FILM AND TV STAR

Now that you're looking at yourself through different eyes, I want you to revisit Chapter One. In that chapter, you wrote down three compliments that you often receive from other people. Just in the span of time that you've spent working your way through this book, I guarantee you that you're getting *new* compliments.

When you make the kinds of changes you've been making, it doesn't go unnoticed. So take a minute to honor that and write down some or all of the new comments you've been getting on the "updated" you:

ONE _____

TWO _____

THREE _____

Once you've written down the new compliments you're getting, transfer them to a Post-it note or into your phone, and keep it by your desk, somewhere you can look at them often. This will be a daily reminder and a celebration of you. The first time you did this, you might have a received a compliment along the lines of "you have beautiful eyes." And you still do. But now that you've started paying more attention to what you're projecting to the world through your self-image, wardrobe, and beauty regimen, your eyes are just a small *part* of the whole fabulous picture that is you and the compliments will start rolling in.

"WHEN YOU RADIATE HAPPINESS FROM WITHIN, NOT ONLY
DO YOU FEEL BEAUTIFUL, YOU FEEL SEXY, TOO."
—TRACEY BREGMAN, EMMY®AWARD-WINNING ACTRESS

ACCEPTING COMPLIMENTS WITH GRACE

While we're on the subject of compliments, let me ask you this: When some-one says, "You look great!" do you automatically start pointing out every reason you think you don't? As in, "I didn't get any sleep last night and I'm getting a zit and this top is from the discount rack and I don't think these jeans are doing anything for my hips and blah, blah, blah . . ." Whoa. Stop right there. If someone gave you a present, would you throw it back at them? Well, that's exactly what a compliment is, a little gift that's intended to brighten your day. Learning to respond graciously to compliments is a bit like re-recording that negative inner dialogue that we've talked about. Except it's a lot easier because all you have to learn are two words. Are you ready? Those two words are *thank you*. This will take some time, but you've earned the praise. Here are some examples to get you started:

> FRIEND: *"What a pretty blouse! It looks gorgeous on you."*
> YOU: *"Thank you!"*
> COWORKER: *"Your hair looks amazing!"*
> YOU: *"Thank you!"*
> HUSBAND: *"Honey, that dress is fantastic! You look beautiful in red!"*
> YOU: *"Thank you!"*

Get the picture? Like everything else you've learned in this book, allowing yourself to feel good about a compliment will take a little time. But you deserve them! When people compliment you, it comes from a good place. They're acknowledging that you've worked to present yourself as the beautiful, strong, confident woman you are. Don't sabotage those moments; embrace and enjoy them.

In committing to the steps I've given you in this book, you've actually made a commitment to yourself. Women tell me all the time, "I would love to dress better but I don't know how." My response is, "I'll show you how." That's why I wrote this book. It's easy to sit around complaining about something you want to change, and then never do anything about it. But it takes real courage and determination to get off your butt, take action, and do the work. And the rewards are sweet! It's so much better to take matters into your own hands and pull yourself out of that safe little rut where you were living, all unhappy about your life and throwing pity parties every day. Now, you've climbed out! Give yourself a pat on the back. Pop open the champagne. Throw your arms around your husband and give him a big kiss, just because.

Speaking of husbands, when I bring my married ladies out for the big reveal after their makeovers, their husbands are literally stunned, in awe, and over-the-moon excited that their wife's "light" has been turned back on. She's sexier than ever because she finally *feels* like the star that she is. I stand there like a proud father, just beaming. And I'm beaming over the progress you've made too. When you like who you are and believe in yourself, there's a domino effect—you feel better about yourself, so your husband sees that in you, and ultimately the energy in the house is different so *everything* is changed. There's a newfound joy and everyone reaps those benefits.

I NOW COMMAND YOU . . .

. . . to create your own style commandment. You're probably thinking, "What? LZ, that's your job!" Well, yes it is, but now that you've learned to fly, I need to nudge you out of the nest. The idea here is to create a commandment that you can put into practice each and every day to help you stay on this new path that you've created for yourself.

Sure, I've given you the keys for success in your wardrobe and appearance, but *you're* the one who has chosen to use those keys to change your life. Now all I'm asking you to do is to keep yourself from falling into old habits.

I don't want to check in with you six months or a year from now and find a messy closet filled with oversized sweatshirts and ratty shoes, with you racing out the door barely having brushed your teeth, much less put on lipstick or added a necklace that complements your top. Not okay. That's what I call surrendering, and on LZ's Style Team, we don't surrender—we win the war of the wardrobe!

So, how do you keep from reverting back to your former ways? You take that extra time at night to prepare your look for the next day, you meditate, you eat healthy, you work out, and you look at yourself in that full-length mirror every morning before you leave the house and say your style mantra out loud. This might feel silly at first, but it's powerful. I'll show you how to write your own style mantra, but first I want to share what works for me.

"RED HIGH HEELS MAKE ME FEEL SEXY . . . AND MY HUSBAND GOES NUTS."
—CRISTINA FERRARE, TV HOST, AUTHOR AND JEWELRY DESIGNER

LZ'S DAILY STYLE MANTRA

Earlier in the book, I shared with you my standard morning routine, and it works really well for me. It took me a while to strike just the right balance, but I've vowed not to rush through my mornings anymore. I create a schedule for my day, and I budget my time for everything—including my social media check-ins. By sticking to my schedule, I give myself just the right amount of time to pay adequate attention to my appearance, whether I'm going to the studio to tape a TV show or not. Another person in my life who does the exact same thing is my older brother, Vincent. He takes such pride in his appearance that he always takes that extra time to pay attention to the details, and his wife, Maria, consistently compliments him on looking so handsome. Vincent in a suit is a homerun.

That said, there are those days, those "special" days when you wake up (you know exactly what I'm talking about) and you're sick. You feel bad. You had the most delicious Mexican dinner the night before and now you feel like crap. Any time I'm bloated, groggy, grumpy, or snotty, I have learned to live by contrary action. I will literally say out loud, "Choose the contrary action!"

So, what does that mean? Well, it means doing the opposite of what I feel like doing. Sure, I'd rather crawl back in bed and pull the covers over my head and watch *The Young and the Restless*, but I already know how that story ends—it ends with nothing changing, nothing happening. Me in bed. Probably eating. No, thanks! Instead, I force myself to get up, go to the gym, take a shower, take care of my business responsibilities, and pull myself together. And when I do, I will be rewarded with new experiences, meeting new people, and who knows what else could be in store?

My dad would always say, "If you walk down the street and fall in a hole, then you walk down the same street and fall in the same hole—what do you do the third time? You choose a different street." There's something about the surprise of doing something different, taking a chance, pushing yourself. The next time you don't feel like facing the world for whatever reason, choose the contrary action, pick a different road, and see what happens.

Your style mantra is like your own little daily check-in, your reminder of why you deserve to be the best version of yourself, and why it's worth the extra little effort it takes to do so. This is meant to solidify your new, gorgeous look so that you truly become one of those women who just make great style seem effortless—because it's second nature to you!

HERE'S AN EXAMPLE OF SOMETHING YOU MIGHT SAY TO YOURSELF:

MIRROR, MIRROR ON THE WALL . . .
I AM DESERVING OF IT ALL.
BEAUTY COMES FROM A PLACE INSIDE,
EVEN WHEN I'M FEELING FRIED.
WATCH OUT WORLD, READY OR NOT,
I'M COMING AT YOU, AND LOOKING HOT!

Hilarious! This still makes me laugh, and hopefully you're laughing too. My point is that you want it to be something that might give you a little chuckle, will empower you, and will remind you to go get 'em every single day, and do it in a really sexy pair of heels . . . because those hot shoes might just be what give you the courage to take a risk that could change your life. This mantra is also a reminder never to deny yourself the endless and amazing possibilities, opportunities, and strokes of genius that good style could bring your way. That mantra, as cheesy as it is, is also to remind you to not take this all so seriously. Looking good and feeling good is a choice and why shouldn't you want to choose to be the best you?

The incomparable Miuccia Prada summed it up so beautifully when she said, "What you wear is how you present yourself to the world, especially today, when human contacts are so quick. Fashion is instant language."

It's so true! Fashion is a form of language, so ask yourself each day what you're saying with your looks. It seems like with all the texting, emailing, voicemailing, and other forms of impersonal "messaging," that we see so much less of each other in today's world. But you know what? That means our appearance is even more important, because when we do have a face-to-face meeting or a power lunch, we've got to look G-O-O-D and make an impression. The old saying that you only get to make a first impression once has never been more relevant than it is now.

Okay, I'll step off the soapbox now and hand the mic over to you. The time has arrived for you to write your style mantra. This can be as short or as long as you need it to be. Write it here, or keep it in your smartphone so you can pull it up anytime, anywhere. But definitely write it down somewhere, because I find that I'll actually remember things better if I write them down. C'mon, you can do this!

MY OWN PERSONAL STYLE MANTRA

_____

_____

_____

THE GOOD, THE BAD, AND THE INSECURE

As you've been transforming yourself and your look and experimenting with new ways to dress, you might have already experienced moments of feeling out of place or a little insecure. This is totally normal. We all have those feelings from time to time, but in those moments, I want you to remember your new style mantra. Tell yourself to just throw your shoulders back, toss your hair around (think: supermodel in slow motion), and realize that if you exude strength, confidence, and power, then everyone will believe you are strong and powerful, even if you're not always convinced.

"THE RIGHT PAIR OF HEELS IS ALL I NEED TO FEEL SEXY AND POWERFUL."
—JULIE BENZ, FILM AND TV ACTRESS

If that's not enough, and you feel like the insecurity is literally taking root in your body, then let me tell you what I do. Very often, when I'm feeling bad about myself, or I'm just down, I will write down a list of five things that I'm grateful for in that moment. This little exercise always pulls me right out of the downward spiral because it reminds me how much I really have. My list changes from day to day, but here is an example of one of my "gratitude lists":

- MY RELATIONSHIP WITH GOD
- MY NEPHEWS, BECAUSE THEY ALWAYS REMIND ME WHAT PURE LOVE IS
- MY BROTHERS, VINCENT AND GREGORY
- THE JAR OF COINS I HAVE ON THE CUPBOARD
- MY AMAZING GROUP OF FRIENDS THAT CELEBRATE ME ON A DAILY BASIS

Now, create your own gratitude list. You'll be surprised by what comes to mind and it will change depending on the moment. The reality is, if you'll just take two or three deep breaths, get out of your head, and drop into your heart with this gratitude list, you'll instantly feel better. Stick it on your bathroom mirror or put it on your nightstand or in your wallet, anywhere, just as a reminder to get you through a tough day

MY GRATITUDE LIST

ONE _____   _____

TWO _____   _____

THREE _____

FOUR _____

FIVE _____

No matter what you're grateful for in your life, I want you to always remember that you are beautiful, you are loved, you have so many good qualities to share with others, and there is only one YOU in the whole, wide world. Trust me; when you focus on the positive, your inner peace will shine through, even if your pants are a little too short or your sweater has a stain on it. Throw those insecurities out the window, babe, because you are dazzling!

THE 1,432,276TH REASON WHY I LOVE WHAT I DO

Yes, there really are that many reasons why I love my job, if not more! One of them is because of something that you're likely experiencing right now, which is a shift in perspective. When you bought this book, who would have guessed that you were actually going to change your perspective on your life so much that you would learn things about yourself that you never knew? You might have thought you bought it for fashion, but once you got inside, you knew this journey was going to be far more than what you put on the outside. I see it all the time. When you make the decision to change the way you look and how you dress, you simply can't help but discover new things about yourself. You've now learned that a well-tailored jacket can change your posture, and will have you standing tall and glowing with confidence and strength. You've discovered that red lipstick not only looks glamorous but makes you feel glamorous. Shapewear has, quite literally, reshaped your entire appearance, and is now the foundation of every new look. You've also learned that looking good doesn't cost a fortune and I've shown you ways to shop within your budget and look like a million bucks.

But these facts, these not-so-subtle changes on the outside, help you tell a different story about yourself. As you try new things and reinvent yourself, your experience becomes different. Your decision to try on something new and change the way the world sees you, and therefore how you see yourself—well, that's what inspires me every day. That's what makes my job so satisfying. #blessed

---

"FEELING SEXY IS FINDING INNER PEACE AND KNOWING THAT I'M
TAKING CARE OF MYSELF, EATING WELL AND STAYING ACTIVE!
IT'S A SUBTLE CONFIDENCE AND EASE!"
DAISY FUENTES, TV PERSONALITY, FASHION MOGUL AND AUTHOR

When you look at yourself completely differently, your inner dialogue begins to change. You might look at yourself now and say, "I like my haircut," or "That lipstick is pretty," or "Look at how nice that outfit looks on me." By reprogramming your inner dialogue, your whole day can change. You look better, you feel better, you like yourself better, and people respond to you better. The women I've made over have always said, "You made my life better."

Like I said in the very beginning of this journey together, it's not just about changing an outfit, it's about stepping outside your comfort zone, finding out who you really are, and then showing that person to the world. If I can get you to do that, then I've done my job.

"BEING LOVED MAKES ME FEEL SEXY."
—JACLYN SMITH, FILM AND TV ACTRESS, FASHION AND HOME DESIGN ICON

TOP FIVE TAKEAWAYS FROM LZ'S TENTH COMMANDMENT

ONE COMPARE AND CONTRAST THE "OLD YOU" TO THE "NEW YOU" IN THE FORM OF A BEFORE-AND-AFTER PHOTO. CELEBRATE THE AMAZING CHANGES YOU'VE MADE!

TWO CREATE YOUR OWN STYLE MANTRA AND USE IT EVERY MORNING, OR IN MOMENTS WHEN YOU NEED INSPIRATION TO LOOK YOUR BEST.

THREE WHEN YOU'RE STUCK IN A RUT OR AFRAID TO STEP OUT OF YOUR COMFORT ZONE, DO SOMETHING DIFFERENT AND CREATE A COMPLETELY NEW EXPERIENCE.

FOUR MAKE A "GRATITUDE LIST."

FIVE ALWAYS REMEMBER THAT YOU ARE BEAUTIFUL, YOU ARE PERFECT, YOU ARE UNIQUE, AND YOU ARE LOVED.

NOW THAT YOU'VE COME TO THE END OF MY BOOK,
YOUR JOURNEY ISN'T OVER—IT'S ALL JUST BEGINNING.
YOU NOW HAVE NEW TOOLS TO CREATE A BEAUTIFUL,
EXCITING, AND PEACEFUL LIFE.

ENJOY IT ALL; ENJOY YOUR MOMENTS!
WITH LOVE,

LAWRENCE & STEVE HARVEY

AFTERWORD BY STEVE HARVEY

The moment I met Lawrence, I felt his passion for style. It's infectious. But it's not just his energy and enthusiasm. This man's got skills. He takes the intimidating world of fashion and makes it accessible for women. Many people don't realize that fashion isn't about what's hot off the runway. It's about what you feel hot in! And that's just what Lawrence teaches women every day.

Each time he's been on my daytime show, he's given our guests a new perspective on how to dress and how to feel beautiful inside and out. It's unbelievable how many women come to us feeling unattractive, women who've basically given up on trying to look good and feel good. They've never treated themselves to a nice dress or indulged in a pair of hot shoes. And it's not that they don't want to. They don't know how to.

Then they meet Lawrence.

He exposes them to looks they never thought they could pull off. He shows them styles they never thought they could afford. He empowers them to take control of their self-image. And you should see these ladies walk out of here. They walk taller. They're smiling from ear to ear. They're beaming with pride and confidence.

I'm a big believer that what you put out there is what you get back. Sure, with these 10 Commandments for a Perfect Wardrobe, Lawrence gives women the tools to look like a million bucks. But he also gives them the chance to feel like a million bucks. And, let's be honest, when you feel great, great things happen.

So, from one author to another, I say keep it going, Lawrence! You're doing important work, my man!

FASHION GLOSSARY

CLOTHING	TOPS

BOATNECK
A wider neckline that is cut directly below the collarbone.

CAMISOLE
A short, loose-fitting undergarment with spaghetti straps, often worn under a sheer top.

CAP SLEEVE
A short sleeve that covers the top of the shoulder and a tiny bit of the very top of the arm.

COWL NECK
A neckline that hangs in draped folds. Also known as a draped neckline.

DÉCOLLETÉ
A low-cut neckline that reveals the neck, shoulders, and upper part of the chest.

FLUTTER SLEEVE
Slightly longer than a cap sleeve, a flutter sleeve has a ruffled effect.

KEYHOLE NECKLINE
This neckline features a small opening or slit
at the front that is closed at the top.

PEASANT BLOUSE
A loose-fitting blouse, usually with a gathered
neckline, that's inspired by traditional
European folk costumes.

SCOOP NECK
A round, usually low neckline.

SHRUG
A close-fitting, cropped cardigan with long or
short sleeves.

TUNIC
A loose-fitting, thigh-length garment that slips
over the head and is worn over pants or
a skirt.

TWINSET
A matching sweater set that includes a
cardigan and a pullover. The pullover is
often sleeveless or short-sleeved.

V-NECK
A V-shaped neckline that can be either low
or high cut.

A-LINE
The name says it all: This is a skirt, dress or top shaped like a capital A. It's narrow at the waist and wider at the hem.

BODICE
The bodice is the upper part of a dress—i.e., not the skirt and not the sleeves but the part that fits around the torso.

EMPIRE WAIST
A waistline that is right under the bustline, above the natural waist.

MAXI DRESS
A floor- or ankle-length dress worn on informal occasions. Maxi dresses are often fitted at the top and loose and flowing at the bottom.

PENCIL SKIRT
A straight skirt that narrows towards the hem, often with a slit or kick pleat at the center back to make walking easier.

SHIFT
A simple, sleeveless dress that hits at the knee or just below. A shift is slim but not form-fitting and does not have a defined waist.

WRAP DRESS
A wrap dress is designed to be wrapped around the body and tied.

CAPRI PANTS
Also known as crop pants, these are pants that are hemmed at mid-calf. They can also be slim-fitting or a looser trouser style.

CIGARETTE PANTS
Slim fitting pants that are narrow through the thigh and have a small leg opening.

DAISY DUKES
Extremely short, form-fitting cut-off denim shorts.

SHORT SHORTS
Shorts with an inseam of four inches or less.

BLAZER
A lightweight tailored jacket that's not part of a suit. A boyfriend blazer is a slightly oversized version of the classic blazer.

BOLERO JACKET
A short, open, cropped jacket that stops below the bustline, with short or long sleeves.

NOTCHED LAPEL
Most often found on blazers and coats, a notched lapel is a lapel with a V-shaped indent between the collar (which goes around the neck) and the lapel (which comes down over the chest).

OVERCOAT
A long, warm coat worn in cold weather.

PEA COAT
A short, double-breasted coat, often made of wool, modeled after those originally worn by sailors.

SHAWL COLLAR
A rolled collar and lapel that's cut in one piece. A shawl collar curves from the back of the neck down to the front closure of a jacket or coat.

SWING COAT
A swing coat is a fuller-cut coat and hangs loose from the shoulders. It can be any length, from the waistline to mid-calf.

BROCADE
A heavy fabric, sometimes with metallic threads, that's woven to produce a slightly raised pattern.

CASHMERE
Fine, lightweight, very soft and warm wool from the Kashmir goat.

CHARMEUSE
A lightweight silk fabric that's satiny to the touch.

JERSEY
A stretch fabric that's knit in a plain stitch without a visible rib. Wrap dresses are often made of matte jersey.

SHANTUNG
A type of fabric, often silk, woven in a heavy, slubby weave.

| CLOTHING | DRESSMAKING TERMS |

BIAS CUT
A piece of clothing is cut on the bias when it's cut diagonally across the grain of the fabric. This means that it's very clingy and drapes over the curves of the body.

DART
A tapered seam that's used to adjust the fit of a garment.

PLEATING
A fold that's made by doubling fabric on itself and stitching it into place. Usually pressed flat but sometimes left unpressed.

RUCHING
Gathered fabric that's used as a decorative effect on dresses, blouses, and skirts.

| ACCESSORIES | SHOES |

ANKLE STRAP PUMP
A pump with a strap that wraps around the ankle.

BIKER BOOT
A mid-calf, pull-on or zip-up, round toe, black leather boot with a low heel and a buckle accent around the ankle.

BOOTIE (AKA ANKLE BOOT)
A boot that only reaches the ankle. Heels come in an assortment of styles and heights.

D'ORSAY PUMP
A pump that has cutaway sides that reveal the arch of the foot.

DRIVING SHOE
A soft loafer in which the sole runs up onto the back of the shoe.

ESPADRILLE WEDGE
A round toe wedge with a canvas or cotton upper and a flexible sole made of rope.

FASHION SNEAKER
A flat, rubber sole, lace-up tennis shoe with a rubber toe cap. There are two distinct styles: high top (extends above ankle) and low top (below the ankle).

GLADIATOR SANDAL
As the name indicates, this is an open toe, flat, multi-strap sandal, with straps extending as low as mid-ankle or as high as mid-calf, and is reminiscent of the ancient Roman gladiators.

GRANNY BOOT
A leather pointed or rounded toe, skinny or thicker short heel boot that laces up to the ankle or mid-calf.

KITTEN HEEL
A small, skinny heel that looks like a miniature stiletto and is usually less than two inches high. Also known as a Sabrina heel.

KNEE-HIGH BOOT
A tall, zip-up boot with a flat, stacked, or stiletto heel.

LOAFER
A leather shoe shaped like a moccasin.

MULE
A shoe that has a closed front and no back.

PLATFORM
A shoe or boot with a very thick sole made of cork, rubber, wood, woven rope, or plastic, and often covered in leather.

PUMP
A classic shoe with a continuous line around the foot that fits tightly enough to stay on without a strap or laces. The only exception is the d'Orsay pump.

RIDING BOOT
A knee-high pull-on or back zip, flat leather boot with a rounded toe.

SANDAL
A style of shoe that leaves most of the upper part of the foot, especially the toes, exposed.

SLINGBACK
A shoe with an open back and strap around the heel to hold it in place.

STILETTO
A very thin high heel.

STRAPPY PUMP
A high-heel, open toe shoe with one or more straps around the toes and ankle.

TOE CLEAVAGE
The partial exposure of the toes by a pair of low-cut shoes.

T-STRAP
A style of shoe that has a strap shaped like a capital T.

WEDGE
A raised heel in which the heel and sole of the shoe are made in one solid block.

Toe Cleavage

CLUTCH
A handheld bag with no shoulder strap; can range from small to large.

CROSSBODY BAG
A smaller bag with a long strap worn across the body that allows you to be hands-free.

EVENING BAG
A small, often decorative bag that's meant to accessorize an evening dress.

FRAME BAG
A handbag with a strong, often angular structure that's built on a metal frame.

HOBO BAG
An unstructured, crescent-shaped handbag with a shoulder strap.

MESSENGER BAG
Very similar to a satchel bag, a large, square-shaped bag with a thick strap meant to be worn across the body.

SHOULDER BAG
A handbag with a strap or straps long enough to be worn over the shoulder.

TOTE BAG
A large, roomy handbag, often with an open top.

BANGLE
A bangle is a bracelet that has no opening or clasp and is put on by sliding it over the hand.

CHANDELIER EARRING
An earring set with a drop suspended like a chandelier. Also known as a drop earring or, if the drop is tear-shaped, a teardrop earring.

CHOKER
A piece of fabric or a necklace that fits snugly around the neck.

CLIP-ON EARRING
An earring that does not pierce the ear.

COCKTAIL RING
A large ring set with real or fake precious or semi-precious stones. Also known as a dinner ring.

CUFF
A rigid bracelet with a narrow opening on one side that is slipped around the wrist.

EARRING CONVERTER
A jewelry attachment that converts earrings for pierced ears into clip-ons.

HOOP EARRING
A circular or oval earring made of a continuous piece of metal that pierces the ear.

PEARL NECKLACE
A strand of pearls worn around your neck; comes in an assortment of lengths including choker (14-16 inches), princess (17-19 inches), matinee (20-24 inches), opera length (26-34 inches), and rope length (45 inches).

PENDANT
A loose hanging piece of jewelry, generally attached to a necklace. The combination is known as a pendant necklace.

STACKED BRACELETS
Multiple bracelets worn on one arm.

STATEMENT NECKLACE
A large, eye-catching necklace.

STUD EARRING
A small earring with no pendant.

MEN'S FASHION GLOSSARY

SHIRTS	CLOTHING

BUTTON-DOWN COLLAR
A collar that's fastened to the shirt with buttons on both points.

Button Down Collar

CAMP SHIRT
A button-front shirt with a collar and no neckband. A camp shirt usually has a straight hem, a boxy cut, and side vents and is worn for more casual occasions. I guarantee you, the Hawaiian shirt in your guy's closet is a camp shirt.

FRENCH CUFF
A shirt cuff that is folded back and fastened with cufflinks.

PLAID SHIRT
A short- or long-sleeve button-up shirt with a crisscross woven pattern.

POLO SHIRT
A casual knitted cotton shirt with a small collar and several buttons at the neck.

CLOTHING | **PANTS/SHORTS**

CARGO SHORTS
Loose-fitting casual shorts that come to just above the knee and have large flap pockets on the thighs.

CHINOS
Chinos are casual pants made from a type of cotton twill that was originally used to make summer uniforms for the army. Also known as khakis.

FLAT-FRONT
Pants with no pleats at the front for a clean, neat look.

BLAZER
A type of jacket that resembles a suit jacket but is worn in more casual situations.

BOMBER JACKET
A short jacket, often leather, that has a zip-up front and an elasticated waist and cuffs.

SPORT COAT
Does not come as part of a suit, and is designed to be worn on its own.

VENT
The slit in the bottom rear of a jacket or at the sides of a camp shirt. Jackets can have a single center vent, two side vents, or no vents.

CHAMBRAY
Lightweight denim cloth.

FLANNEL
A soft woven fabric that's been brushed for additional warmth and comfort.

GABARDINE
A tightly woven wool with vertical twill lines.

LINEN
Cloth that is woven from flax. Linen is usually worn during the summer.

PINSTRIPE
Evenly spaced, very thin white stripes woven into a dark fabric. Pinstripes are associated with formal business attire.

SEERSUCKER
A cotton or synthetic fabric that has a puckered surface and is usually striped.

ACCESSORIES   SHOES

BIKER BOOT
A mid-calf, pull-on or zip-up, round toe, black leather boot with a low heel and a buckle accent around the ankle.

BLUCHER
A blucher is more casual than an oxford.

BOAT SHOE
A type of loafer with a flexible rubber sole and heel to provide traction on boat decks. Also known as topsider.

CAP TOE BOOT
A leather boot that laces up the front with a stitched design, separating the toe from the rest of the boot.

CHUKKA BOOT
A suede or leather shoe that comes up to the ankle and laces through two or three pairs of eyelets.

FASHION SNEAKER
A flat, rubber sole, lace-up tennis shoe with a rubber toe cap. There are two distinct styles: high top (extends above ankle) and low top (below the ankle).

LOAFER
A slip-on leather shoe shaped like a moccasin.

OXFORD
A type of laced shoe in which the shoelace eyelet tabs are stitched under the vamp. An oxford is more formal than a blucher.

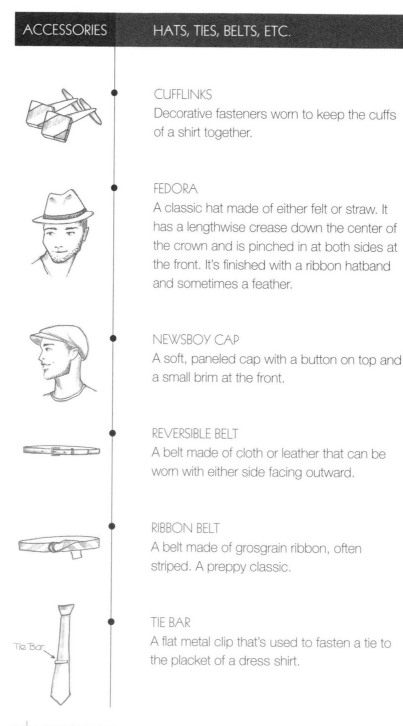

CUFFLINKS
Decorative fasteners worn to keep the cuffs of a shirt together.

FEDORA
A classic hat made of either felt or straw. It has a lengthwise crease down the center of the crown and is pinched in at both sides at the front. It's finished with a ribbon hatband and sometimes a feather.

NEWSBOY CAP
A soft, paneled cap with a button on top and a small brim at the front.

REVERSIBLE BELT
A belt made of cloth or leather that can be worn with either side facing outward.

RIBBON BELT
A belt made of grosgrain ribbon, often striped. A preppy classic.

TIE BAR
A flat metal clip that's used to fasten a tie to the placket of a dress shirt.

Tie Bar

WINDSOR KNOT
A method of tying a necktie that produces a wide, symmetrical triangular knot.

WOVEN BELT
A fabric or leather belt that's braided.

WOVEN TIE
A thick, silk, textured tie with a pattern or design.

LZ'S MAKEOVERS

"BEING A CANCER SURVIVOR HAS TAUGHT ME TO TRULY APPRECIATE
THE BLESSINGS IN MY LIFE. RECEIVING A MAKEOVER FROM YOU WAS ONE
OF THE MOST WONDERFUL EXPERIENCES I HAVE EVER HAD.
LAWRENCE, YOU HELD MY HAND AND GUIDED ME THROUGH THE ENTIRE
MAKEOVER PROCESS. YOU NEVER ONCE MADE ME FEEL OUT OF PLACE, EVEN
WHEN YOU WERE HELPING ME OUT OF MY CLOTHES IN THE DRESSING ROOM.
YOU WERE AN ABSOLUTE GENTLEMAN. I HAVE NEVER FELT
SO AMAZING, SASSY AND CHIC!"

SARAH VANCE
24 YEARS OLD, NEW MOM, CANCER SURVIVOR

"LAWRENCE, I TRULY AM SO BLESSED AND I WILL NEVER FORGET YOU!
YOU'RE A VERY KIND, SWEET AND CARING MAN. YOU HAVE CHANGED MY LIFE
AND YOU MADE ME A LADY. YOU ALSO MADE ME
FEEL BEAUTIFUL. I WLL NEVER FORGET YOU."

JENNIFER QUINTANILLA
42 YEARS OLD, MOTHER OF TWO, OPERATING ROOM SCRUB NURSE

"THANK YOU LAWRENCE (AND YOUR TEAM) FOR MAKING ME FEEL
LIKE A STAR. YOU TURNED ME FROM AN OUTDATED, FRIZZY-HAIRED
MOUSE INTO A BLONDE BOMBSHELL. NOW WHEN I'M WEARY AND FEELING
LIKE GIVING UP, YOUR WORDS, 'KEEP YOUR GLAM UP' ECHO. YOU UPLIFTED ME
WITH YOUR TALENT, CARE AND JOYFUL DEDICATION. THANKS TO YOU, LAW-
RENCE, I ALWAYS TAKE A LITTLE TIME TO 'KEEP MY GLAM UP'."

KAREN SMITH
55 YEARS OLD, MOTHER OF SIX, HOUSEWIFE